ABOUT THE AUTHOR

Sally Morgan was born in Malaysia but grew up in England. She studied Literature and Classics at university. After graduating, she worked as a bookseller and as an editor before becoming a full-time writer. She is the author of many books including *Dream Big* and the My Best Friend series. Sally lives in Minneapolis with her husband and two children.

EMMA RADUCANU

A LiFe STORY

Sally Morgan
Illustrated by **Mike Phillips**

SCHOLASTIC

To my champions, Lily and Daisy.

First published by Scholastic Non Fiction in the UK, 2021
Euston House, 24 Eversholt Street, London, NW1 1DB
Scholastic Ireland, 89E Lagan Road, Dublin Industrial Estate, Glasnevin,
Dublin, D11 HP5F

SCHOLASTIC and associated logos are trademarks and/or
registered trademarks of Scholastic Inc.

Text © Sally Morgan, 2021
Inside illustrations by Mike Philips
in the style of Sarah Papworth © Scholastic, 2021

ISBN 978 0702 31664 7

A CIP catalogue record for this book is available from the British Library.

Printed in the UK by CPI Group UK (Ltd), Croydon, CR0 4YY
Paper made from wood grown in sustainable forests and other
controlled sources.

1 3 5 7 9 10 8 6 4 2

www.scholastic.co.uk

CONTENTS

INTRODUCTION

Every year in June and July, tennis lovers around the globe are glued to their screens watching the greatest players on the planet battle it out at The Championships, Wimbledon. And people in Britain, even those for whom tennis isn't a favourite sport, all go a bit tennis mad.

Television programmes send correspondents to broadcast live from the tournament, covering everything from just how many portions of strawberries and cream will be sold to how long fans have queued to get into the grounds, and even which Hollywood celebrities have flown in to watch the action.

Inside the grounds, there is a carnival atmosphere with people hoping to catch sight of their favourite players and maybe get an autograph or a selfie. For British fans, The

Championships, Wimbledon are extra special as many people watch in the hope of seeing a British player win.

For many players, Wimbledon is the highlight of the tennis calendar as it is the oldest of the four major Grand Slam tournaments, the only one to still be played on grass and arguably the most prestigious. Young players dream of one day playing at Wimbledon and lifting one of the famous trophies into the air.

WHAT DOES IT MEAN TO WIN A GRAND SLAM?

The Grand Slam tournaments are the four most important tennis tournaments held each year: the 'majors'. These tournaments offer the highest prize money and greatest number of points towards players' rankings. Only the very highest ranked players are invited to take part in these tournaments.

THE GRAND SLAM TOURNAMENTS:

Australian Open: January (hard court)

French Open, also known as Roland Garros:
May-June (clay court)

Wimbledon: June-July (grass court)

US Open: August-September (hard court)

Achieving a Grand Slam can mean a player winning all four Grand Slam tournaments in a year or in their lifetime; a 'career Grand Slam'.

Wimbledon, The Championships

For many British fans, seeing a player win at Wimbledon is their ultimate dream. For years this was a dream that seemed impossible to fulfil. Britain had produced great tennis players, some of whom had come very close to winning, but it took until 2013, when Andy Murray became the first British man to win the Men's singles competition since 1936. It was a wonderful moment, but afterwards fans looked to the women's game for a champion. A British woman hadn't won the Wimbledon trophy since Virginia Wade in 1977. Many people wondered how long they would have to wait until a British woman lifted the famous Venus Rosewater Dish again.

THE VENUS ROSEWATER DISH

The Venus Rosewater Dish is awarded to the winner of the Women's Singles Championship. It is made of solid silver with a gold-plated rim and is engraved with a classical scene.

Even though winners are awarded the dish, they aren't allowed to keep it, instead, they receive a ¾-size replica to take home. The winner's name is engraved on the trophy and joins the names of all the previous winners since it was first awarded to a British player named Blanche Bingley in 1886. Bingley went on to play in a further twelve Wimbledon finals and won a total of six times.

For one player, eighteen-year-old A-level student, Emma Raducanu, the 2021 Championships were a dream come true. Having taken time off at the beginning of 2021 to study for her exams, Emma returned to tennis hungry to win and continue her journey as a professional tennis player. Emma had planned to take part in Wimbledon as she had in previous years, playing in the qualifying rounds of the competition with the hope of making it into the main draw, but this year was different. Triumphing in a number of smaller tournaments before Wimbledon, she had shown people just how much potential she had. Because of this she was offered a place in the main draw without having to qualify.

A Fairy Tale Tournament

Emma was delighted to accept the invitation. She knew she was talented and that she was playing better than she ever had before, but with a ranking of 338 Emma couldn't have expected what happened next and neither could anyone else. She stormed through her first match, then her second and her third, beating two players ranked in the top fifty on her way into the fourth round. Emma won all three of her matches without even dropping a set. When she won her third match against Romanian Sorana Cirstea she could hardly believe what she had just done.

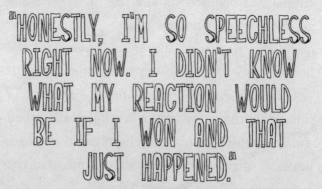

"HONESTLY, I'M SO SPEECHLESS RIGHT NOW. I DIDN'T KNOW WHAT MY REACTION WOULD BE IF I WON AND THAT JUST HAPPENED."

Emma Raducanu

But it was certainly no fluke. Emma outplayed each player with her strong serve and powerful ground strokes. She was fast across the court and planned each point with meticulous precision.

With each match Emma won, more people began to take notice. Fans realized that they were witnessing the debut of a future champion, a British player with the potential to win Grand Slam tournaments. As interest in Emma grew, so did her social media following, which shot up to more than 250,000, but Emma tried to block it out. Although she was aware of how excited people were for her, with people starting to recognize her around the grounds, Emma stayed away from her phone in order to focus on playing and recovering between matches.

Fourth Round

The atmosphere was electric on 4 July 2021 when Emma Raducanu and Australian Ajla Tomljanovic walked on to Court One to play the fourth-round match that would decide who would go through to the quarter final. The crowd was excited to watch great tennis but even more, everyone was excited to see Emma do well. Joining the fans in the stadium, millions more watched from home with celebrities and even members of the royal family tweeting their support.

Emma had yet to lose a set and had impressed people with her athletic and aggressive game, her powerful serve and strong ground strokes. She had impressed everyone too with by staying calm under pressure. More importantly, Emma had captured people's imaginations with her thrilling journey through the tournament. It was a story that made people believe overnight success and even a little magic was somehow possible.

But it wasn't magic, and Emma's success hadn't come overnight. Her progress had been quick, but Emma had trained for many years to get to this point in her career. She had woken up early to train before school, and trained as soon as school was over. She had missed out on trips and parties to travel to tournaments and given up her many other hobbies in order to devote almost every free moment she had to the game. And she hadn't done it on her own either. Although she was alone on court, Emma had a whole team of people behind her, her coach, her physiotherapist, the many people at the tennis clubs she had trained at growing up and, most importantly of all, her parents whose love, sacrifice and support had been with her from the beginning. Emma was under a lot of pressure, but she was used to it. She had been brought up to come through difficulties and meet problems with a positive attitude. Her attitude had helped her succeed in tennis and balance her demanding training and tournament schedule with studying for her GCSEs and her A-levels.

But even though Emma had worked hard and had the support of her family, her team and even the crowd in the stadium, the events of the past few days came rushing in. The match against Ajla Tomljanovic was tough, with hard-fought points and long rallies, this and the stifling heat on Court One had Emma struggling to catch her breath. Three games into the second set even the crowd began to notice that Emma was no longer striding confidently across the court, but holding her stomach. The encouraging cheers that met Emma after every point, transformed into murmurs of concern. Emma's parents looked on nervously from the stands, unable to help.

Emma knew she couldn't go on. She signalled the umpire that she needed to speak to a trainer. Soon afterwards, the umpire announced, "Miss Raducanu is not able to continue the match."

It was a shock to everyone watching. Emma's triumphant journey through the championship had come to an end. But Emma and her team had made the decision to protect her mental health.

Emma may have felt alone in her struggle on court, but she was not the first elite athlete to pull out of a competition to protect their mental health in 2021 and she wouldn't be the last.

A SUMMER OF SPEAKING OUT

In May 2021, four-time Grand Slam champion, Japan's Naomi Osaka, withdrew from the French Open in the second round. She'd asked to be excused from the press conferences held after matches as she believed they would

NAOMI OSAKA

be damaging to her mental health. The organizers warned that if she didn't attend she could be expelled from the tournament and risk being banned from taking part in future Grand Slams. Naomi felt she had no choice but to withdraw. Afterwards, Naomi shared a statement:

"The truth is that I have suffered long bouts of depression since the US Open in 2018 and I have had a really hard time coping with that ... Though the tennis press has always been kind to me (and I wanna apologize especially to all the cool journalists who I may have hurt), I am not a natural public speaker and get huge waves of anxiety before I speak to the world's media ...

So here in Paris I was already feeling vulnerable and anxious so I thought it was better to exercise self-care and skip the press conferences."

Some journalists with little experience of elite sports condemned Naomi, saying that to compete at the highest level, people need to be able to carry on no matter how they are feeling. Journalists with more experience and fellow athletes rushed to Naomi's defence, pointing out how brave she was to speak out about her mental health instead of pushing through it or withdrawing due to a made-up injury as many before had felt forced to do.

"I DO HOPE THAT PEOPLE CAN RELATE AND UNDERSTAND IT'S O.K. TO NOT BE O.K., AND IT'S O.K. TO TALK

ABOUT IT. THERE ARE PEOPLE WHO CAN HELP, AND THERE IS USUALLY LIGHT AT THE END OF ANY TUNNEL."

Naomi Osaka, Time Magazine, 2021

Later in July 2021, four-time Olympic gold medallist, five-time World Champion, gymnastics superstar, Simone Biles, made the following statement on social media after having difficulties in the qualifying rounds of the Tokyo Olympic games:

SIMONE BILES

"I TRULY DO FEEL LIKE I HAVE THE WEIGHT OF THE WORLD ON MY SHOULDERS

"AT TIMES. I KNOW I BRUSH IT OFF AND MAKE IT SEEM LIKE PRESSURE DOESN'T AFFECT ME BUT DAMN SOMETIMES IT'S HARD HAHAHA! THE OLYMPICS IS NO JOKE!"

The very next day Simone walked off the competition floor and USA gymnastics said: "After further medical evaluation, Simone Biles has withdrawn from the final individual all-around competition at the Tokyo Olympic Games, in order to focus on her mental health,"

Simone put this down to the 'twisties', when a gymnast loses the sense of where they are in the air. She knew it would be dangerous to continue and made the decision to let her team take her place until she felt able to compete.

Simone recovered enough to take part in the beam final, taking away a bronze medal. But she did more than that. By being honest about her experience, she showed that even the most consistent performers who seem to smile through everything can have struggles that people know nothing about. Simone was inspired by Naomi Osaka speaking so frankly about her mental health. She felt it was an important conversation for everyone to be having, stating: "I say put mental health first. Because if you don't, then you're not going to enjoy your sport and you're not going to succeed as much as you want to. So it's OK sometimes to even sit out the big competitions to focus on yourself, because it shows how strong of a competitor and person that you really are – rather than just battle through it."

For Emma, the media reaction was swift, with some questioning whether Emma had the 'mental toughness' to play at such a high level. Athletes with experience in elite sports soon rushed to Emma's defence – including premiership footballer, Marcus Rashford, who tweeted "It happened to me playing for the national team in U16s against Wales. I remember it to this day. No explanation for it and it never happened again. You should be very proud of yourself. The country is proud of you … Onwards and upwards."

Emma was glad of the support, telling Vogue:

"I WAS FEELING LIKE I LET PEOPLE DOWN, SO FOR HIM TO REASSURE ME LIKE THAT – I WAS EXTREMELY GRATEFUL."

And the country was proud of Emma – of how well she had played and of how she had conducted herself on and off the court. And far from letting anybody down, Emma not only inspired people with her story, but also with her courage in speaking out about what happened to her.

Only the Beginning

Emma's performance at Wimbledon, making it to the fourth round in her first ever Grand Slam tournament, had boosted her ranking from 338 to 179 and shown people just what a formidable player she was. This meant she would be able to continue to compete in high-level major tournaments. For Emma it was just the beginning.

Her performance at Wimbledon left tennis fans around the world wondering who Emma Raducanu was and how she managed to achieve such a feat in such a short time. And what, after such an achievement, would she go on to do next?

FIRST STEPS

Although Emma Raducanu competes for Great Britain on the tennis court, she was not actually born in the United Kingdom. She was born in Toronto, Canada, on 13 November 2002. Her father, Ian, is originally from Bucharest in Romania and her mother, Renee, is from Shenyang, in China. Emma's parents moved to the United Kingdom when she was two years old. The family made the move for work and also because they thought it would be an exciting place for Emma to grow up. Emma and her family settled in Bromley in Southeast London. This leafy suburb is an easy journey to central London, but also has lots of green spaces such as parks and more importantly, tennis clubs.

Picking up a Racket

Bromley was the perfect place for Emma's parents who both work in finance and love to stay active. One of the ways Emma's parents liked to get out and about was to play tennis. When Emma was five years old, Ian and Renee started taking lessons at a park near their home. Rather than leave her at home with a babysitter, they brought Emma with them, along with her bicycle. As they played, Emma cycled around the outside of the court. Sometimes her parents' coach would lay out cones for her to race around and sometimes she would have a go with a racket herself. Emma wasn't sure how much she liked the game at first, but she kept trying and eventually her parents decided to enrol her in her own lessons.

School Days

Around this time, Emma had also started going to school. She attended a school named Bickley Primary School in Bromley. Emma liked school a lot and worked hard. Emma's mother and father both came from academic families and so they believed that school work was very important. Emma's favourite subject at school was maths as she liked solving calculations as though they were puzzles. As well as maths, Emma liked PE. Bickley Primary School had an excellent PE department where students could try lots of different sports from football and netball to boxing and even golf! Another sport Emma got to play at school was tennis.

Even though Emma was only in reception class, her teachers were impressed with how good she was and thought she showed promise. Whereas most children in her class were just learning to hold a racket and make any sort of contact with the ball, Emma was not only able to hit the ball over the net but could even hold short rallies, where several shots are played back and forth between the players. Emma was good at running, too. She was one of the fastest in her class and won the sprint at sports day almost every year.

GETTING A GRIP

One of the first things a young tennis player needs to learn is how to hold a racket properly.

1. Put your racket flat on the ground.

2. Place the hand you prefer to throw and

catch with over the handle over your racket facing downward.

3. Position your hand so that your thumb and forefinger form a v shape.

4. Pick up your racket as though it were a frying pan.

Confidence Boost

Emma enjoyed school and was good at her lessons, but she was very shy. Even when Emma knew the answer to her teacher's questions, she was never the first to put her hand up in class. To help Emma feel more confident, Emma's parents enrolled her in lots of out-of-school activities. As well as tennis, Emma's mother, Renee, enrolled her in ballet, hoping that performing may give her more confidence, but that wasn't enough for her father, Ian. He wanted his daughter to try a variety of activities such as horse riding, so that she could develop a diverse set of skills. He also hoped she would find something she could be really passionate about.

"I WAS INITIALLY IN BALLET, THEN MY DAD HIJACKED ME FROM BALLET AND THREW ME INTO EVERY SPORT YOU COULD IMAGINE. I WAS DOING HORSE RIDING, SWIMMING,

TAP DANCING, BASKETBALL, SKIING, GOLF AND FROM THE AGE OF FIVE TO EIGHT, I WAS GO-KARTING,"

says Emma.

Emma started go-karting when she was five years old, learning to drive a small petrol-driven car around Streatham Bus Garage. Eventually Emma moved on to a go-karting club with a real track.

When Emma was six years old, she joined the tennis performance coaching programme at the Parklangley Club in Beckenham. The Parklangley Club had excellent facilities with both indoor and outdoor tennis courts including grass courts just like the ones at Wimbledon. The Parklangley Club also had an excellent youth programme that worked with players as young as three and four years old.

The club also had lots of experienced coaches. While Emma was at the Parklangley Club she trained with a coach named Harry Bushnell. Harry said that Emma stood out, in spite of not saying very much when she was on court.

Even at such a young age Emma's talent shone through. She had good technique, but she was good tactically too, able to work out ways to read her opponent in order to win.

"I'D SAY SOMETHING LIKE 'DO YOU UNDERSTAND EMMA?' — AND SHE WOULD JUST NOD!"

Harry Bushnell, tennis coach

It wasn't just Emma's talent that stood out, it was her self-discipline too. Even though she led a busy life with lots of hobbies, Emma was never late for her early morning practice. Emma practised at 7 a.m. so that she could fit in training before school.

STARTING YOUNG?

While five may sound young to start playing tennis, some very successful tennis players started much younger.

Tennis-playing super-star sisters Venus and Serena Williams started playing tennis with their father when they were just three years old, as did British Wimbledon Champion Andy Murray.

Romanian tennis star, Simona Halep, first stepped onto the court when she was four years old but didn't start to play regularly until she was six. Whereas Li Na, Emma's idol and China's first ever Grand Slam singles champion first picked up a racket aged eight as did eight-time Wimbledon Champion, Roger Federer.

Many professional tennis coaches recommend players start learning to play tennis at aged five or six, so Emma might have made the best possible start.

PLAYING TO WIN

Emma may not have been the youngest when she started playing tennis, but she was a quick learner and it wasn't long before her coaches recommended that she start taking part in tournaments. Competing was a great way for Emma to use what she had learned in her lessons and see how far she had come. It turns out she had come a long way. Emma first took part in tournaments at her club and eventually tried local and regional competitions.

JUNIOR TENNIS

To make sure the game isn't too challenging, young tennis players compete on smaller courts with lower nets and with different balls.

Eight and under – Players compete on courts

that are one quarter of the size of normal tennis courts and with special mini tennis nets that are lower than normal tennis nets. Players play with red balls. Red balls are bigger than standard tennis balls and have less air inside them, which makes them bounce more slowly. The slower bounce allows younger players the time to get in the right position in order to hit the ball properly.

Nine and under – Players compete on courts that are three quarters of the size of standard tennis courts. This is achieved by moving the baseline forward by about thirty centimetres as well as moving each of the side lines inwards by the same amount. The smaller court means young players don't have to hit the ball as far. Players also compete with orange balls. Orange balls have half as much air as standard yellow balls.

Ten and under – Players play on full-sized tennis courts and play with green balls. Green balls are the same size as the standard yellow balls but do not bounce quite as high or fast because they have only three quarters of the amount of air inside them.

The Lawn Tennis Association

The tournaments Emma competed in were overseen by an organization called the Lawn Tennis Association (LTA). The LTA manage all areas of tennis in Great Britain, from training the nation's best players at the National Tennis Centre in London to encouraging people new to the sport to step onto the court. The Lawn Tennis Association is a charity that was founded in 1888 and trains coaches

DUCHESS OF CAMBRIDGE

as well as players and organizes tournaments for players to compete against one another. The patron of the Lawn Tennis Association is Catherine, Duchess of Cambridge, who often attends their events.

Playing Up

To begin with, Emma competed in club tournaments, but as her skills improved she began to play in tournaments organized by other clubs. Even though Emma was only six years old, she often played in Under-eights tournaments. This meant she frequently had to play against children much older than she was. In 2009, Emma took part in the Under Eights Girls Championship at Bromley Tennis Centre. She had to compete against players who were well over a year older than she was and who had much more experience on court. If Emma was nervous, she didn't let it show. She stepped out onto the court and won.

Winning tournaments not only helped boost Emma's confidence, it also improved her rating as a player. As Emma's rating improved it meant she could enter more tournaments and play against tougher players.

Ratings and Rankings

The Lawn Tennis Association uses a rating system to measure how well players play the game. Players can improve their rating by playing in tournaments. A player's rating determines which grade of tournament they can enter. The higher the rating, the higher the grade of tournament they can compete in. Junior players' ratings are calculated from tournaments played within their age group and within the age group above.

Tennis rankings are used to understand how well you play the game and whether or not you are suited to a particular tournament. A player works their way up the ranks by playing and winning tournaments. A player's ranking is calculated by adding up the points they earn in singles and doubles tournaments. Rankings also determine where a player is 'seeded' within a tournament. Seeding helps divide the best players up, so that they don't end up playing against one another right at the beginning of a tournament. Spreading the top players' matches out across the early stages ensures that they don't eliminate each other at the start of the competition.

Growing Through the Grades

Young players like Emma learn how to play in tennis lessons, but they learn how to compete at tournaments. Players learn most from competing against players of a similar standard to themselves. To help players know which tournaments they are suited to, tournaments are given grades.

GRADE SEVEN: Local competitions held at a player's own tennis club or club nearby. These tournaments help a player to improve their rating but don't contribute to their ranking.

GRADE SIX: This level is open to all and involves playing matches against players within their age group. As with grade seven, winning grade six tournaments can improve a player's rating but not their ranking.

GRADE FIVE: These competitions are higher, at club or county level. Players can improve both their rating and their ranking at these tournaments. Winning a grade five tournament can add 75 points to a player's ranking.

GRADE FOUR: These are county level competitions at which players can improve both their ratings and their rankings. Winning a grade four tournament can add 125 points to a player's ranking.

GRADE THREE: These are regional competitions that take place throughout the year. Emma's region was the southeast, which includes Surrey, Middlesex, Kent and Sussex. Players can improve their ratings and their rankings in these competitions. Winning a grade three tournament can add 250 points to a player's ranking.

GRADE TWO: These are national level competitions, which count towards ratings and rankings. Winning a grade two tournament can add 750 points to a player's ranking.

GRADE ONE: These are the highest level of junior competition. Players can enter these tournaments by invitation only. Winning a Grade One tournament can add 1,000 points to your ranking.

The Start of a Streak

From April 2010, Emma competed more often. Even though she was only seven years old, she competed in the nine-and-under age group. In July, she won the Sundridge Park Junior Open and went on to win the Kent County Closed Junior Open in straight sets – none of her opponents managed to win a single set against her – in August.

The more Emma competed and won the more she liked it. In October 2010, she took part in her first regional tournament organized by the Lawn Tennis Association. In a regional tournament, Emma had to play against all of the best tennis players in her age category who lived in Kent, Surrey, Sussex and Middlesex. Emma triumphed. Once again seeing off players older than herself to lift the trophy without dropping a set.

KNOW THE SCORE

In tennis a match is broken up into points, games and sets. A point is won when the opposing player cannot return the ball over the net back into the other half of the court. The ball mustn't bounce more than once on either side of the net or the point is lost.

A player needs at least four winning shots to take a game. Both players begin at zero, which in tennis is called 'love'. The first point takes a player to fifteen, the second to thirty, the third to forty. If the player is now two points clear of their opponent, winning this next shot – game point – gives them the game. If both players make it to forty, this is called 'deuce'.

To win the game at deuce a player needs to win two consecutive points against their opponent to take the game. To take a set, a player must win six games and must have won by at least two games more than their opponent.

In women's tennis, players must take two sets out of three to win. When the next winning shot will win the match, it is called 'match point'.

Emma's coaches and parents were pleased with her progress and believed she could do even more and so they entered her in her first national tournament. In December 2010, Emma played in the LTA Winter national Tournament at the White Horse Tennis Centre in Oxfordshire. Emma played well, but lost in the quarter finals to the player who went on to win the championship.

Off the Court

Emma worked hard at school and she played hard with her hobbies, applying her focus and determination to each of them, but sometimes she needed a break. During the holidays, Emma and her parents often went to visit family in China and Romania. Emma particularly enjoyed visiting her grandmother in Bucharest. Emma's grandmother, or *mamaia*, always cooked her delicious food whenever she came to stay with her.

Emma also visited her mother's family in Shenyang, Liaoning province, China, and got to practise at a local tennis school when she was there. When she was in China, Emma also liked to play table tennis, using her skills in tennis to help her play. Tian Fangzheng, head of the table tennis club where Emma often played described Emma as an "outstanding" player with plenty of energy, claiming that "When all the other kids were tired, she was not."

Emma was busy and probably didn't

MOTHER

44

have as much time to watch television as most children her age. But one thing she did make sure to watch was tennis. Emma loved to watch the world's best players compete and hoped that one day she could be just like them. Emma's favourite player to watch was Li Na from China. Emma admire Li Na's powerful serve and how athletic and aggressive she was on court. She also admired Na's mentality and how she seemed to never complain.

PLAYER PROFILE: LI NA

Born: 26 February 1982 Wuhan, China
Nationality: Chinese
Height: 5' 7"
Plays: Right-handed
Highest WTA ranking: 2
Won nine WTA singles titles, including two grand slam titles. Li won the 2011 French Open and the 2014 Australian Open.

"I JUST KEEP FIGHTING AND TRY TO BE THE LAST ONE STANDING."

Going National

By now, Emma had developed a taste for winning. She had competed and won at club, county and at regional level but now she wanted to win a national tournament. But winning at this level proved to be easier said than done. Throughout 2011, Emma competed in national tournaments around the country including the LTA Winter National Tournament in Bolton, UK, and the LTA

British National Championship at the National Tennis Centre in Roehampton, London. Emma played well and fought hard on court but she was unable to reach higher than runner up.

Just because Emma didn't win, didn't mean she wasn't getting better, but it meant she had more to learn, and she was a quick learner. As well as training at the Parklangley Club, Emma was selected to attend LTA regional training camps at the Bromley Tennis Centre. Emma listened to her coaches and while she was still shy, she took on their feedback to improve her game.

Even though tennis was taking up more and more of Emma's time, her father still wanted her to keep up her other hobbies too. Emma thinks that throwing herself into lots of different activities helped her work on her motor skills and her coordination. It helped her confidence too.

When Emma was nine

MOTOCROSS

years old, she took up motocross. Motocross is a sport where people learn to ride motorcycles as fast as they can over rough and muddy terrain. Emma had her own Kawasaki crosser bike and although she was still very shy she was fierce competition for all the boys in her group, and they were mostly boys.

Emma didn't let this stop her, she was used to being the only girl – it had been the same in go-karting, too. Emma said in an interview she thought it was 'pretty cool' and made her feel proud when she was able to beat them.

"FOR EXAMPLE, ONE TIME, MY MOTOCROSS TEACHER WAS LIKE, RIGHT, WE'RE GOING TO DO PRESS-UPS. I WAS THE ONLY ONE WHO COULD DO IT,

SO I WAS PROUD OF MYSELF FOR THAT."

Emma Raducanu, Vogue, 2021

Fighting Spirit

Emma was strong and determined and her hard work paid off. In February 2012, Emma travelled to South Yorkshire to play in the LTA Winter National Event at the Graves Tennis Centre. Emma played well and made it all the way to the final. In the final, Emma lost the first set, seven games to two. Emma could have let the lost set shake her confidence and affect the rest of her game, but she didn't. Instead Emma put the lost set to one side and came back to win the next two and her first national under-nine girls singles tournament!

GETTING SERIOUS

When Emma was ten years old, she started playing tennis at Bromley Tennis Centre. Bromley Tennis Centre is a state-of-the-art tennis facility in Orpington, Kent. Emma had attended camps and played tournaments at Bromley, but now she began training there full-time. Emma impressed her coaches with her grit and determination. She was known for being a good listener and eager to try new things to improve her game.

Emma had won a national title, but she continued to compete at a regional and local level. Even though she had only just turned ten, Emma competed in the 2012 Kent County tournament in the twelve-and-under age group and won. Emma didn't win every tournament she played in, but she always learned something from her opponents.

GREAT GROUND STROKES: FOREHAND DRIVE

The first stroke most players learn is the forehand. With practice this simple stroke can be refined into a formidable tool.

When you first learn, experiment holding your racket with one or both of your hands to see what works best for you.

1. Stand, facing your opponent, with your knees bent and your feet shoulder-width apart.

2. Watch the ball as it approaches.

3. If you are right-handed, turn your shoulders to the right, swinging your racket behind you.

4. Step forward towards the ball and rotate your shoulders to swing your racket to meet it.

5. When the ball is in front of you, strike the ball with the centre of your racket strings.

6. Your shoulders should continue to rotate as your arm swings through the ball from low to high.

7. Complete your swing when your racket is over your left shoulder. This is called following through.

Stepping onto the World Stage

In 2013, Emma travelled to France to take part in her first international tennis tournament. Emma competed in the Tennis Europe 11 and Under Event in Bressuire, France, and won. It was her first taste of international success. It was a big step up for Emma, but there was a big step up coming closer to home, too.

A New School

When she was in year six, Emma's parents had to decide where she would go to school for year seven. Emma spent a lot of her spare time playing tennis, but her parents made sure she didn't neglect her studies. They wanted Emma to do well in school so she could choose what she wanted to do when she grew up. Emma's parents believed that their daughter was a talented tennis player and wanted her to do well, but they knew there were no guarantees. Injury or other circumstances could make a future in tennis disappear at any time.

Emma's parents chose a school called Newstead Wood. Newstead Wood was a selective school, which meant that most of the students who went there had to pass an exam to get in. Newstead Wood was an excellent school with a strong academic background, perfect for Emma who loved to be challenged by her schoolwork. But that wasn't the only thing the Raducanus liked about it. Newstead Wood was just a minute's walk to the Bromley Tennis Centre. This was ideal. Being so close to the tennis centre meant that Emma could train before school started at 8.45 a.m. and get there quickly for squad training after school was done for the day.

A Winning Formula

Even though the tennis centre was close, Emma would still have to juggle her schoolwork with her tennis, especially now she was playing in international tournaments. Thankfully her school was used to that. Newstead Wood had experience with working around the schedule of an elite athlete as they were also the school chosen by Dina Asher-Smith. Dina studied at Newstead Wood from 2008 until 2014 while training to be an elite sprinter. Dina went on to become the fastest British woman of all time. While at Newstead Wood, teachers helped Dina fit her sprint training around her schoolwork. At Newstead Dina managed to get three As in her A-levels as well as train hard enough to be selected for the 2013 World Championships in Moscow as part of the Great British 4 x 100 metre relay team – they came away with a bronze medal.

Playing with Friends

Emma made friends playing tennis as well as at school. She spent so much time playing tennis and taking part in tournaments that it was inevitable that she would sometimes have to play her friends

SECONDARY SCHOOL

in competitions. This was difficult, but Emma always tried her hardest. Emma and her friends knew they would still be friends no matter who won.

In May 2014, Emma took part in the Nike 12 and Under LTA Clay Court Tennis championship. Emma made it all the way to the final, but lost to a player she had played many times named Indianna Spink. Emma took the loss in her stride and stepped out on court alongside Indianna to play in the doubles tournament where the pair proved to be unbeatable taking home both a medal and a trophy.

In April 2014, Emma played in the 12 and Under Braga Open Tournament in Portugal. Emma played well, even managing to defeat her best friend in the semi-final. Emma was confident in her abilities and told a television interviewer that she was going to try her hardest in the final and give it her best shot. Emma did just that, winning her second international competition.

Reaching for a Dream

Emma enjoyed travelling to tournaments and was beginning to realize what becoming a professional tennis player might be like. Emma wondered if it might be something she could do when she was older. In August, she finished as runner-up in the 12 and Under National Championship in Dorset. After the match, Emma was asked by a journalist whether she dreamed of being a Grand Slam champion for Great Britain, just like Andy Murray. Emma said that she did.

"I KNOW IT'S REALLY HARD WORK, BUT HOPEFULLY IF I WORK ON MY GAME AND REALLY PULL IT TOGETHER THEN MAYBE IT WILL HAPPEN ONE DAY."

Emma Raducanu

PLAYER PROFILE: ANDY MURRAY

Born: 15 May 1987, Glasgow, Scotland

Nationality: British

Height: 6' 3"

Plays: right-handed

Highest ATP ranking: 1

Highest UK ranking: 1

Andy Murray played his first tournament as an under-ten junior at Dunblane Sports Club in Scotland and went on to become Britain's first male Grand Slam champion in 76 years. He won the US Open in 2012 and 2016. He also became the first British male in 77 years to win the Wimbledon Championships in 2013. Andy lifted the famous Wimbledon Trophy again in 2016.

"I DON'T PLAY IN ANY TOURNAMENTS TO COME SECOND BEST."

Playing for Great Britain

It wasn't just interviewers that had started to notice Emma, the LTA was starting to be interested too. The LTA saw not only how well Emma played but also how cool she stayed under pressure. In November 2014, the LTA selected Emma to play for the national team in the twelve and under Winter European Cup. Emma proved to be a great choice and won almost all of her singles and doubles matches. Emma and her team brought home a bronze medal from the tournament.

An Inspiring Family

Emma's life was getting very busy, but Emma didn't mind hard work. Emma puts this down to her mother's Chinese background, which she says has made her very resilient. Whenever she found her schoolwork hard, her mother would remind her of her cousins in China and how much harder their work was than the schoolwork she was expected to do. In order to complete their schoolwork, Emma's cousins sometimes studied for twelve or thirteen hours a day. Emma was inspired by how hard her cousins worked and wanted to do the same.

Family was very important for Emma's parents and while living far away was sometimes hard, they travelled to visit them whenever they could. Emma enjoyed visiting her family and she also enjoyed trying all the delicious foods. In China,

Emma loved to eat hot pot, but wasn't able to enjoy some of the spicier foods that her mother and her cousins liked.

When they couldn't travel there, Emma spoke to her family in China often and was able to do so in Mandarin. Emma's mother, Renee, spoke to Emma in Mandarin from when she was very little and so Emma picked the language up quickly. This made talking to her family in China much easier. Learning Mandarin also meant Emma could have secret chats with her mum without her dad being able to understand what they were saying to one another! Emma learned to speak Romanian, too, so that she could speak to her grandmother in Bucharest.

When Life Gives You Oranges

In December 2014, Emma ended the year in the sunshine when she entered the Orange Bowl 12 and Under tournament in Miami, Florida. At the Orange Bowl, Emma got to compete against players, not just from Great Britain or Europe, but from all over the world. Unfortunately, Emma lost in the first round to a player named Whitney Osuigwe. But Emma didn't let the defeat get her down. Unlike many other tournaments at the Orange Bowl, players continue to compete against one another, even after losing early in the competition. While Whitney Osuigwe went on to win the tournament, Emma went on to win her next ten matches and came out in fifth place overall.

COACHING A CHAMPION

Back at Bromley Tennis Centre, Emma began working with a performance coach named Alastair Filmer. A performance coach is one who doesn't just help a player improve the various strokes they are working on. Performance coaches look at all aspects of a young player's career and help come up with a programme to help them become the best they can be.

As well as building up Emma's skills and competency on the court, Alastair worked with Emma on her warrior mentality so that she could stay calm but ruthless on the court. Alastair also focused on Emma's mental resilience so that she could get through difficult moments in a match, working on drills and exercises to train Emma not to just survive those moments but to thrive in them and even use them to her advantage.

Father Knows Best

As well as working with players, performance coaches also work with their families. Emma's father, Ian, was keen to get involved. Ian wanted Emma to become one of the best returners in the world and wanted her to be able to

FATHER

change direction on any ball. Ian was involved in every aspect of her training from hitting balls with her in his spare time to working with her performance coach on what he wanted Emma to focus on. Ian could see his daughter had talent and he wanted to do everything he could and make sure Emma could achieve her full potential. Ian even strung her rackets himself and sent her to tournaments with new strings for her rackets that he had pre-cut so that her racket would be just the way she liked it when she stepped onto the court. Ian came to Emma's coaches with tips and suggestions as well as looking for guidance on how to help Emma be the best she could be.

Together with Emma and her family, Emma's coach came up with a bespoke development plan to how she would approach the busy twelve-and-under tour. Emma's coach kept a spreadsheet of what they were going to work on each day to build on her skills. Emma was a natural athlete, but also a hard worker. She held herself to a high standard in everything that she did. Emma's coach knew she had an excellent timing and good backhand and was brilliant at being able to move up the court.

And because school was so close, she was able to take time out of school for mini sessions to work on different aspects of her game.

GREAT GROUND STROKES: BACKHAND DRIVE

The second stroke a player learns is the backhand drive. Backhands can be tougher to master than the forehand because you're hitting the ball on the opposite side to your dominant hand. Practise this shot until it's a reliable weapon to defeat your opponent.

1. Hold your racket with both hands. Stand, facing your opponent with your knees bent and your feet shoulder-width apart.

2. Watch the ball as it comes towards you. If the ball is approaching your back-hand side, your left side if you are right-handed, turn your shoulders to the left, swinging your racket behind you and transferring your weight to your left foot.

3. As the ball becomes closer, step towards it with your right foot and rotate your shoulder to bring your racket around towards the ball.

4. Strike the ball with the centre of your racket while continuing to swing your racket until it is over your right shoulder.

Emma's Weekly Schedule

Monday: no tennis day. School from 8.35 a.m. until 3.35 p.m.

Tuesday – Friday: 7 a.m. tennis with coach. School from 8.35 a.m. until 3.35 p.m.

Break times and lunch: personal court time to practise skills.

After school: squad training.

Saturday and Sunday: tournaments and/or strength and conditioning.

As well as training with her performance coach, Emma played and trained with the squad at the Bromley Tennis Centre. This gave her the opportunity to practise against players of different ages and abilities. Emma played against players older than herself in order to stretch her skills. Each week Emma practised her tennis 12-14 hours as well as doing four to five hours of strength and conditioning work.

Strength and Conditioning

As well as working with her performance coach, Emma also worked on her strength and conditioning. She had a strength and conditioning coach from when she was just seven years old. Emma's first strength and conditioning coach was named Suzanne Williams. Suzanne remembers Emma's athleticism from when she first met her at the Parklangley Club. When Emma was eight years old, Suzanne challenged her to see how many press-ups she could do in a minute. Emma immediately dropped to the floor and performed forty-eight perfect push-ups without bending her knees or breaking her form in any way. Suzanne was shocked as this was more than she had expected, and more than some much older athletes were capable of.

When Emma was twelve, she started working with a coach named Gareth Shelbourne who worked in Sutton, Surrey. Strength and conditioning coaches use a combination of strength work, such as weight and resistance training, and aerobic exercise, such as running, to help improve an athlete's performance and stamina. These specialist coaches can also help prevent injury by teaching an athlete how to move around quickly and safely. Strength and conditioning coaches take into consideration an athlete's age and physical ability to create a plan to help them achieve their physical goals. In tennis, strength and conditioning coaches can work to improve an athlete's footwork, agility, balance, explosiveness and speed. A good strength and conditioning coach helps athletes to understand their bodies and how to get them to move the way they want them to safely. With young students, these coaches work with parents too so that they can help their young athlete apply what they are learning outside of their sessions.

Turning Training into Trophies

Emma soon turned all of her hard work training into trophies. In July 2015, she took part in the 18th Team Bath CoMpete Open Tennis Festival. Emma, who was still only twelve years old, proved that she had the skills to compete and win not only in the Under 14 girls singles competition, but also the singles tournament for Under 16 girls.

A Dream Come True

In August 2015, Emma got the chance to take part in the HSBC 14 and under Road to Wimbledon Tournament at Wimbledon. Emma worked her way through the southeast regional qualifying matches in June. After the final qualifying match Emma said,

> "IT FEELS GREAT BECAUSE I'VE ALWAYS WANTED TO PLAY AT WIMBLEDON ... IT'S WHAT YOU AIM FOR."

The HSBC Road to Wimbledon Tournament gave juniors the chance to follow in the footsteps of their favourite players and step out onto the famous grass courts at the All England Club at Wimbledon. While they were there, the young athletes got to compete against one another but were also given the opportunity to see the famous Wimbledon trophies – trophies that they hoped one day to win.

THE CHAMPIONSHIPS, WIMBLEDON

Wimbledon is home to the oldest and arguably the most famous tennis tournament in the world. For two weeks in July every summer the greatest names in tennis fight out on Wimbledon's famous grass courts. Wimbledon is the only major tournament played on grass.

The first Wimbledon Championship took place in 1877, but this tournament was only for men as women were not allowed to compete. The first women's championship was held in 1884. Wimbledon is also the championship with the strictest dress code. Players competing at Wimbledon are expected to wear all white.

Even the trainers on their feet have to
be white.

Wimbledon Champions include Virginia Wade,
Venus and Serena Williams, Roger Federer, and
Andy Murray.

ON THE SURFACE

Unlike many other sports, tennis can be played
on different surfaces and professional players
are expected to be able to play equally well on
all of them even though they can make a big
difference to how the ball bounces and how a
player can move around the court.

GRASS COURTS

Players have to be fast on grass courts as balls
bounce much lower to the ground meaning the
player has to get to them quickly. Players also

have to prepare for the unexpected, because even well-maintained grass courts can be a little uneven meaning the ball can often bounce off in unpredictable directions.

Find them at: fancy tennis clubs. Grass courts are expensive to maintain and cannot be used year-round. The world's most famous grass courts can be found at Wimbledon.

CLAY COURTS

Players have to prepare for long rallies on clay courts because the crushed stone or brick surface allows the ball to bounce higher and more slowly allowing players time to get in just the right position to return the ball.

Find them at: tennis clubs. The most famous clay courts are at the French Open in Paris.

HARD COURTS

Hard courts are made from concrete or asphalt, the same material used to make roads and school playgrounds. The concrete or asphalt is then coated with layers of acrylic to cushion and even the surface. Play on hard courts is usually faster than on clay courts but not as fast as on grass courts. Hard courts tend to be more even so players can predict how the ball will bounce and prepare for their next shot. These courts can be tough on players as they run around the court.

Find them at: sports clubs and your local park. Both the US and Australian Open are played on hard courts.

OTHER SURFACES

If you are lucky enough to have a local park with tennis courts, they may be hard courts like the ones described above, or they may even be asphalt like your school playground. Asphalt is cheap and easy to maintain, which makes it ideal for outdoor courts that get a lot of use.

Indoor sports centres often have synthetic courts. Synthetic courts are like carpets that can be rolled out over an existing gym floor. Synthetic courts are ideal in situations where the space is needed for lots of different sports. These courts are pre-marked with court markings, but be careful when you step off them because you can get a static shock.

THE CLIMB TO THE TOP

As Emma's success grew, so did her confidence. While she may still have been shy in the classroom, Emma was confident in her abilities on court. She had proved herself to be one of Great Britain's most talented young tennis players and because of this, she was invited to take part in training camps held at the National Tennis Centre in Roehampton, London. These training camps bring together players who the Lawn Tennis Association believe have the potential to become champions. The players invited to attend these camps are given access to the tennis centre's cutting-edge facilities and are coached by some of the world's best coaches, lifestyle advisors and sports medicine professionals.

A Big Celebration

In November 2015, Emma celebrated her

thirteenth birthday by doing the two things she loved most, playing tennis and winning! Playing in the 14 and Under Tennis Europe competition, Emma won both the singles and doubles events. She had been looking forward to this birthday because a player had to be at least thirteen to take part in International Tennis Federation (ITF) Under 18 competitions. Emma's first ITF Under 18 competition was the Nike Junior International in Liverpool. As a newcomer to these events, Emma entered the tournament unseeded (see page 38), but she soon proved herself a force to be reckoned with. Despite being younger than all the other players, not to mention smaller and less experienced, Emma made it through to the final and won against the tournament's top seed.

INTERNATIONAL TENNIS FEDERATION

The International Tennis Federation was founded in 1913 and it is the governing body of world tennis. The ITF regulates tennis competitions around the world and maintains and enforces the rules of tennis agreed by all its members. The ITF organizes and oversees tournaments for lower ranked players who have just turned professional and also calculates rankings.

Fine Tuning Talent

Emma was getting stronger and winning more competitions, but that didn't mean she could relax. Emma had high standards for herself and always felt like she could do better and learn more. Her parents had high standards for Emma too and expected her to put in the hours and do her best without complaining.

Emma worked hard with her coaches perfecting her serve, making it stronger and faster. She worked on sharpening up her returns, trying to make them faster and lower. Emma practised against the best players at the Bromley Tennis Centre always looking to learn something to improve her game to make her reaction times quicker and cross the court more swiftly and aggressively. During each session her coach would work with her on what she could do better and what they needed to work on next. Emma was always listening and always ready to learn, but she enjoyed herself too. Laughing with her friends and with her coaches, updating her Instagram and being teased for taking too many selfies and not training hard enough. Nothing could be further from the truth.

Emma also continued to compete and prove she was a contender. In December 2016, Emma returned to Miami to compete in the Under 14 Orange Bowl improving on her performance the previous year by bringing home third place. From the beginning, Emma had shown that she could hold her own against players older than herself, and the LTA had faith that she could do just that when they chose her to play for her country, selecting her as one of just four players to make up the Under 18 girls tennis team to compete against the United States in a tournament called the Maureen Connolly Cup.

In July 2017, Emma returned to Wimbledon to play in the junior girls singles competition. Emma won her first-round match but lost her second. The tournament was an excellent learning experience not least because she got to meet one of her favourite tennis players of all time, Roger Federer.

PLAYER PROFILE: ROGER FEDERER

Born: 8 August 1981, Basel, Switzerland
Nationality: Swiss
Height: 6' 1"
Plays: Right-handed
Highest ATP ranking: 1

First man to win twenty Grand Slam singles titles and considered one of the greatest tennis players of all time.

FEDERER

"YOU ALWAYS WANT TO WIN. THAT IS WHY YOU PLAY TENNIS, BECAUSE YOU LOVE THE SPORT AND TRY TO BE THE BEST YOU CAN AT IT."

Fellow athletes at the Bromley Tennis Centre were excited to watch one of their own play at Wimbledon, not only because they trained alongside her but also because she was an exciting player to watch. She was fast on the court and had a strong serve. Emma was known for playing to win and being ruthless against her opponents when it counted.

At the end of 2017 Emma took centre stage at the Royal Albert Hall when she took part in the Champions Tennis Event in partnership with the charity SportsAid. At the Royal Albert Hall Emma got to play in front of a big crowd alongside

British tennis legends such as Greg Rusedski and Tim Henman and international champions such as Pat Rafter and Mark Philippoussis.

PLAYER PROFILE: GREG RUSEDSKI

Born: 6 September 1973, Montreal, Canada
Nationality: British
Height: 6' 4"
Plays: Left-handed
Highest ATP ranking: 4
Highest UK ranking: 1

Greg Rusedski was born in Montreal, Canada and moved to the United Kingdom in 1995. Greg's career highlights include reaching the Wimbledon quarter final and the final of the US Open in 1997. Greg Rusedski retired from

professional tennis in 2007 and now works
with the LTA and as a sports journalist.

GREG RUSEDSKI

"IT'S ABOUT YOU. IF YOU
WIN, IT'S YOU; IF YOU
LOSE, IT'S YOU. BLACK AND
WHITE. NOWHERE TO HIDE."

PLAYER PROFILE: TIM HENMAN

Born: 6 September 1974, Oxfordshire, United Kingdom

Nationality: British

Height: 6' 1"

Plays: Right-handed

Highest ATP ranking: 4

Highest UK ranking: 1

Tim Henman was born in Oxfordshire in the United Kingdom and grew up to become one of the great hopes of British tennis to the point where a hill near Court One at Wimbledon is still referred to as Henman Hill as it was where crowds of fans gathered to watch him play on the big screen.

Tim reached the semi-finals in three out of the four Grand Slam tournaments including the Wimbledon semi-final four times. Tim retired in 2007 and now works as a tennis commentator and journalist.

TIM HENMAN

"I'LL KEEP DOING THE RIGHT THINGS AND THE RESULTS WILL COME."

SPORTS AID

SportsAid is a charity that supports promising young athletes between the ages of twelve and eighteen as they aim to reach the top in their sports. SportsAid has helped thousands of athletes achieve their goals including Mo Farah, Jessica Ennis-Hill and Tanni Grey-Thompson.

At the SportsAid event at the Royal Albert Hall, Emma got to stand alongside some of the greatest players Britain had ever produced. Even though Emma was only fifteen it was becoming clear that she may soon become one of them.

Top Girl

In 2018, Emma began to dominate the junior tennis circuit, playing and winning in two international tournaments in India. Emma won match after match. As Emma won, she rose up the ranks becoming the number one ranked junior tennis player in Great Britain.

Ten years after first picking up a racket, Emma had risen through the ranks to become the best junior female player in Great Britain. Emma had made it to number one by pushing herself to work harder and challenging herself to reach higher, but now that she was number one it seemed like there was nowhere left to go. At just fifteen years old Emma had reached the top of the junior rankings, and rather than stay there, Emma and her father wanted to find a new and greater challenge. For Emma, this could mean only one thing, leaving junior tennis behind and trying her hand against professionals.

GOING PRO

· ·

Going professional was a big step. It meant playing in her first professional International Tennis Federation (ITF) tournament. Emma had done well in junior tournaments, but in professional tournaments she would be playing against athletes who were not only older and more experienced, but for whom tennis was their entire lives. Emma still had her schoolwork to focus on.

But taking part in a professional tournament isn't as simple as showing up with your racket to a Grand Slam and wanting to play. It's actually pretty complicated. As Emma was new to the professional circuit she would have to do well in smaller ITF tournaments first before she would be allowed to enter bigger tournaments on the Women's Tennis Association Tour or Grand Slam Tournaments. Even in those smaller tournaments she wouldn't be allowed into the main draw. The main draw is reserved for the highest-ranking players who have applied to compete. Without a ranking Emma had to play in the qualifying draw. In the qualifying draw, the lower-ranked players and new players like Emma have to win a series of three or four qualifying matches in order to move on and play in the rest of the tournament. The process is called a draw because when organizers first put together their playing schedule, player's names would be pulled out of, or 'drawn', from a hat.

Professional Debut

In spring Emma travelled to Nanjing, China, to make her professional debut in the qualifying draw for ITF $15K Tournament held there in March. Emma won her first match easily, without losing a single game. She made it to the third qualifying round where she was defeated by a more experienced player. But Emma didn't let this defeat discourage her. Instead she put it behind her and started afresh in her second ITF $15K tournament held in the same city right afterwards. This time she made it through all of her qualifying matches. Once in the main draw of the competition, Emma made it all the way through to the quarter finals.

This was a great start. Emma had shown she had what it took to make it through the qualifying rounds to the main draw and even the quarter finals in a professional tournament. For Emma this meant the hard work had been worth it, and that she knew if she continued to put in the effort she would soon be in the finals and maybe even winning. It turned out it wouldn't take her long.

A Hot Streak

In May, Emma took part in her third ITF professional tournament in the ITF $15k tournament in Tiberius, Israel. Despite extreme heat from the desert sun, Emma made it through the qualifying rounds of the tournament easily. She didn't struggle in the main draw either, defeating opponent after opponent until she found herself playing in the final and winning without losing a set.

ITF 15k TITLE

Winning a tournament like this at fifteen years old put Emma on the radar as a player to watch out for in the future. It also meant that she received the $15k prize money, which would be a big help in contributing to the expenses that come with playing high-level tennis. These expenses include coaching, equipment and foreign travel. As well as money, Emma also won points that would contribute to her first ever WTA ranking.

How Tennis Rankings Work

In women's tennis, rankings are awarded based on the number of points a player has won in the previous fifty-two weeks. Points are awarded based on how far players reach in each tournament they compete in and are based on their best results in a maximum of sixteen tournaments.

Emma's win in Israel as well as her performance in Nanjing meant that she had accumulated 14 points towards her ranking. Some tournaments are worth more than others, a player can win 2,000 points for winning a Grand Slam tournament.

In May 2018, Emma's first WTA ranking was 885. It wasn't high, but she was on her way.

A Tale of Two Wimbledons

As Emma was only fifteen, it meant that even though she played on the professional circuit she was still eligible to compete on the junior circuit too. This meant that in 2018, Emma entered not one but two Wimbledon tournaments – the women's singles competition and girls' singles competition. In the women's singles competition Emma lost in the first qualifying round, but it was a great experience as the match was even shown on the BBC.

Emma did better in the girls' competition, working her way through her opponents all the way up to the quarter finals, including beating Canadian tennis player, Leylah Fernandez in the second round (see page 156). Emma's performance in the junior competition got her some attention from sports journalists who singled her out as one to watch in the future, noting that she had a big serve and strong returns that often left her opponents reeling.

HOW TO SERVE

Every point in tennis begins with a player serving the ball to their opponent on the other side of the net. Players take it in turns to serve the ball for an entire game.

With a great serve, a player can win the point by serving the ball so quickly and powerfully their opponent isn't able to hit it. This is called an ace.

1. If you are right-handed, position yourself facing the net on the baseline of the court, slightly to the right of the centre line. Step back your right leg so that your body turns until it's side-on to the net. Left-handers should switch to mirror these positions.

2. With your ball in your left hand, slowly raise your arm above your head as you look to where you want the ball to land on the other side of the court. Swing your right arm, with your racket down and back, taking your weight onto your back foot.

3. When your left arm is fully extended, release the ball into the air so that it flies high enough for you to have to reach for it with your racket.

4. Reach for the ball with your racket. Strike the ball as it starts to fall to the ground, while transferring your weight from your back foot to your front foot. Try to keep your arm and wrist relaxed as you make contact with the ball.

5. After hitting the ball, allow your racket arm to continue to swing across your body until it ends up at waist height on your left side. This is called a follow through.

If you don't quite get your serve over the net or inside the lines, you get another chance at the point with a second serve. If this serve misses the mark, it's called a double fault and your opponent wins the point.

A Juggling Act

But balancing both the junior and ITF tour with studying for her GCSEs was tricky. Thankfully, Emma's school worked with her, allowing her time off to travel to tournaments and helping her fit her assignments around her training. Emma and her parents had also made the decision that Emma would only compete in tournaments that didn't interfere with school too much. This was tough and Emma sometimes got frustrated that she couldn't attend as many tournaments as older players who no longer went to school or those who had opted to be home schooled. Emma also got frustrated that tennis meant that she missed out on fun school things too. In order to play in the Wimbledon Girls' singles tournament, Emma had to miss out on her school's German exchange trip with her friends. Emma hoped the sacrifice would be worth it.

Emma could see her game improving. In training, Emma had started working with a new coach called Matt James. Matt was impressed with Emma's willingness to learn and her fearlessness on court. As he watched her compete he could see how adaptable she was in a game and how she would learn from difficult moments and play through them. At the beginning of September 2018, Emma took part in the Junior US Open, making it all the way through to the quarter finals.

Emma continued on the ITF circuit, taking part in the Lisbon Women's Open in Portugal in September and the GD Tennis Cup in Antalya, Turkey, in October. In Portugal, Emma lost in her second qualifying round, but in Antalya Emma was in the main draw. She played well, winning each of her matches without dropping a single game and taking home the title, the points and the prize money. Emma played in tournaments closer to home too. At the end of October Emma made it through to the semi-final of her first ITF 25K tournament, the GB Pro-Series in Liverpool.

Money Matters

Taking part in tournaments on both the junior and professional ITF circuit wasn't just tough to balance with school work, it was also very expensive, even with the prize money she was winning. Coaching at this level was costly as was travelling to tournaments and paying for hotels. Thankfully, help was at hand.

As well as overseeing tournaments and coaching in the United Kingdom, the LTA also offers scholarship programmes. The LTA Pro Scholarship Programme offers support to players the LTA believes are most likely to reach a top 100 ranking in five years. Emma's playing record had proven that she was a strong player. Her victory in Turkey and performance in Liverpool had Emma climbing up the ranks to 700, but she still had a long way to go to reach her dream of becoming a top-ranked player. Emma hoped that the LTA may be able to help her get there. In order to be considered for the LTA Pro Scholarship Programme, players not only need to be excellent players, they also need to be between sixteen and twenty-four years old. Emma turned sixteen in November 2018, and was selected for the programme. As well as providing financial support to players, the scholarship programme gave players access to some of the best coaches, medical experts and facilities in the game.

With the LTA Scholarship Programme Emma had a strong network of people around her to help her improve her game. It also meant she had enough money behind her that she didn't have to worry about travelling to tournaments and taking her coaches along with her. All she had to think about was the tennis. But none of this would matter at all if she wasn't prepared to put in the work, but Emma was. She trained before and after school and whenever she could fit it in during the day.

"THANKS TO THIS PROGRAMME, I HAVE BEEN ABLE TO TAILOR MY TRAINING AROUND MY INDIVIDUAL NEEDS AS I HAVE BEEN IN FULL TIME EDUCATION. PUTTING A TEAM AROUND ME THAT UNDERSTOOD THIS WAS VITAL AND BECAUSE OF IT I HAVE BEEN ABLE TO PROGRESS QUICKLY."

Emma Raducanu

In March 2019, Emma took part in an ITF $15K event in Tel Aviv, Israel, making it all the way through to the quarter final before losing to an Italian player named Corinna Dentoni. At the beginning of April she took part in an ITF 25k event in Bolton, in the United Kingdom, making it to the semi-final before losing to British player, and fellow member of the LTS Pro Scholarship Programme, Jodie Burrage.

Time Out

In May 2019, Emma took time out to sit her GCSE exams. Emma had studied for these exams both at school, home and while she was travelling. Emma took everything she needed with her as she was determined to do well.

"I WOULD SAY I HAVE HIGH STANDARDS OF MYSELF. THAT'S HELPED ME GET TO WHERE I AM IN TERMS OF TENNIS AND ALSO IN TERMS OF SCHOOL RESULTS."

The time out was worth it. In August, Emma found out her results; she got three 9s, three 8s and an A in further maths.

With her exams complete, Emma and her family needed to decide whether they wanted her to continue with school or concentrate on tennis full time. Many players quit school or make the decision to continue their studies online, but Emma and her family were pleased with how she had done at Newstead Wood and wanted her to continue. They believed that while tennis was Emma's main goal, school was important and getting good qualifications would help her in the future if tennis didn't work out the way they hoped it would.

Prime Assistance

In November 2019, Emma got further help towards her career when she was selected to receive the Amazon Prime Video Future Talent Award. As part of the award, Emma received £60,000 to put towards her coaching and career development over the next two years. As well as money, Emma received one on one mentorship from Wimbledon Champion, Andy Murray (see page 58). Andy Murray worked with Amazon on the award because he knew first-hand how hard moving from juniors to becoming a professional could be, as well as what it could cost.

Rise Up

The hard work and help from the LTA and Amazon Prime Video paid off. In December 2019, Emma travelled to India to take part in two ITF 25k tournaments. In the first tournament in Solapur, Emma was knocked out in the second round by British player and fellow LTA Pro Scholarship Programme member, Katie Boulter. The following week however Emma blitzed her way through two qualifying matches in an ITF 25K tournament in Pune, India. After qualifying, Emma didn't break her stride, winning another two matches and getting to the quarter final without losing a set.

In the final, Emma had a tougher time against British player Naiktha Bains. Losing the first set by three games to six. Emma needed to draw on what she had learned about how to stay strong during difficult moments in matches. She fought back to win the next two sets, and the tournament.

With each match and tournament Emma won, she racked up points to contribute to her ranking and as her ranking increased so did her eligibility to play in tournaments that could win her even more points. By the end of 2019, Emma had risen to number 374 and was ready to continue.

A BUMP IN THE ROAD

Emma had had a great year in 2019, not only on the court but at school too, passing her GCSEs with flying colours. In 2020, Emma hoped to build on that success by playing in more tournaments and studying for her first year of A-levels. With the LTA Scholarship Programme and the Amazon Prime Video Future Talent Award, it didn't look like anything would be able to stop her. Unfortunately, the world had other plans.

In February 2020, Emma played in an LTA GB Pro-series in Sunderland in the United Kingdom where she finished as runner up, losing in the final to Bulgarian Viktoriya Tomova. Emma also found the time to learn to drive and passed her driving test, but any freedom Emma was to feel on the road was short lived. Tournaments and training filled her schedule in the following months, but Emma didn't get to play in any of them and nor did anyone else. In March 2020, the rest of the ITF tour was cancelled. There were no tournaments, no travel and even coaching became very difficult.

Virus Stops Play

This was because of the spread of a highly contagious virus called COVID-19. This virus was first discovered in Wuhan, China, in 2019 and quickly spread across the world.

COVID-19 affected people in different ways. When infected with COVID-19, some people fell ill very quickly with flu-like symptoms such as a high fever and a cough and breathing difficulties, some patients also reported a loss of taste and smell. Some people, especially older people and people with health conditions that made them more vulnerable to infection got very ill and needed to be treated in hospital. Many of these people were not able to recover from the virus and died.

When the virus was first discovered, scientists weren't sure how it was transmitted or how to treat it effectively. As more people became infected with the virus, hospitals and healthcare systems risked becoming overwhelmed. In order to prevent this from happening, governments around the world including the United Kingdom introduced various restrictions to help slow the spread. Leaders hoped that slowing the spread would take the pressure off hospitals and give scientists the time they needed to learn about the virus and come up with medicines to treat the virus and to formulate a vaccine to prevent people from catching it in the first place.

Lockdown

In the United Kingdom these restrictions included limiting the number of people allowed to enter the country and preventing people from travelling abroad. As well as restricting travel abroad, the UK government also introduced something called a 'lockdown'.

"FROM THIS EVENING I MUST GIVE THE BRITISH

PEOPLE A VERY SIMPLE INSTRUCTION — YOU MUST STAY AT HOME."

Prime Minister Boris Johnson

Under these government restrictions people were only allowed to leave their home to go to work (if they were unable to work from home), shop for food or essentials, exercise, or provide care for someone in need. The government hoped these measures would help slow the spread of the virus and take the pressure off the healthcare service.

For Emma, like for many young people unless their parents were essential workers, this meant she couldn't go to school, but instead had to study for her A-levels at home. For Emma it also meant she was unable to leave the house to go to training and it also meant that tennis tournaments in the United Kingdom were cancelled, and even if they were taking place abroad, Emma would be unable to compete. Emma had hoped that 2020 would be a year in which she could work on her skills, increase her experience competing and build on the successes of the previous year, but like many people Emma's plans had changed.

Emma did not despair. She threw herself into the things she could do, such as studying for her A-levels, exercising by running around her neighbourhood and playing tennis with her dad in the street.

In May 2020, the government announced that the lockdown had slowed the spread of the virus enough to lift some of the restrictions and, while things couldn't get back to normal just yet, people would now be allowed to do more of the things they needed to do outside of the home. For Emma, this meant competing.

In May, the LTA announced that they would be resuming competitions at the National Tennis Centre and eventually at centres across the country. Unlike tournaments Emma had competed in before, due to COVID-19 restrictions the events at the National Tennis Centre did not allow spectators, but that did not mean they weren't exciting or challenging. The LTA put on these events to help tennis players keep up with their training and practise competing.

Emma was thrilled to be able to able to play and compete again and couldn't wait to get on court. She took part in a competition called the Premier British Tour, which brought together some of the best players in the country. Emma proved that she hadn't lost any of her edge in lockdown, winning the first week and eventually the entire tour.

In August, Emma proved once again that she had not lost any of her competitive edge, winning the UK Pro Tennis classic week, fighting her way back from a set down against player Jodie Burrage and winning the final set ten games to eight.

Battle of the Brits

As well as individual competitions, the LTA also organized team tennis events. In July, Emma competed in a competition called the St James' Place Battle of the Brits Team Tennis competition. The Battle of the Brits consisted of two teams, the Union Jacks versus the British

Bulldogs. Emma was selected to be a member of the British Bulldogs, which included British number two men's player Kyle Edmund and British number one women's player Johanna Konta. It was a great experience, as the youngest member of the team, Emma got to play against and alongside some of the greatest British tennis players around. Emma did well, even beating two-time Wimbledon Champion Andy Murray in mixed doubles.

Teams competed in a mix of singles, doubles and mixed doubles matches. Each win won the team points, the team that was the first to accumulate 60 points won the title of Battle of the Brits Team Champions. It was a fun event, but with so many great tennis players trained to win, competition was still fierce. Fans were able to watch on YouTube or Facebook or on BBC iPlayer. The British Bulldogs won with 65 points to the Union Jacks' 45.

Emma was pleased to find she had not lost her edge in lockdown, in fact in some ways her game had improved. After a singles win against Union Jack, Jodie Burrage, Emma said:

"REALLY PLEASED WITH THE IMPROVEMENTS I MADE IN LOCKDOWN, THE FOREHAND ESPECIALLY AND THE RETURN OF SERVE. I'M PLAYING AGGRESSIVELY AND MENTALLY I'M REALLY STRONG AT THE MOMENT."

Emma Raducanu

In December, Emma played in the British Tour Masters event held at the National Tennis Centre in London and won the title before rejoining the British Bulldogs for the Battle of the Brits Premier League of Tennis.

The year 2020 had been a difficult year. Many people had lost loved ones to the pandemic and some people lost their jobs. Some found the lockdown restrictions very lonely and isolating.

In many ways Emma had been lucky. She had

done well in national competitions, but it was not the same as competing on the international stage. Growing up she had watched her idols travelling around the world competing and winning tournaments, lifting Grand Slam trophies and enjoying everything else that came with it. In 2019, Emma had begun to see what was in her future before COVID-19 and the events of 2020 brought it grinding to a halt.

When 2020 finally drew to a close, people all over the world hoped that 2021 would see things getting back to the way they had been before people had ever heard of COVID-19 and lockdowns and if that didn't happen, they hoped that things would at least be better. Researchers had formulated vaccines that looked as though they were able to prevent people from getting the virus. These vaccines had worked well in trials and scientists hoped that once given them, people could start to get back to their daily lives.

Back to Work

As well as the virus and lockdowns, Emma had a lot on her mind at the start of 2021. It was an important year for her. After a year of interrupted schooling, she was due to sit her A-level examinations in April. When Emma finished school she wanted to continue her professional tennis career, but if that didn't work out the way she hoped it would, Emma wanted to work in financial services like her parents. In order to be able to do this Emma needed good results to secure a place on a university course. Emma was studying for A-levels in Economics and in Maths.

Emma's studying was made a little easier by the fact that she enjoyed her subjects. Emma found economics fascinating and even said in an interview that alongside sports superstars Daniel Ricardo of Formula One and basketball legend Michael Jordan, a dream dinner guest would be Chartered Financial Analyst and television economics expert, Tom Keene.

"I THINK MY PARENTS JUST THINK I'M CRAZY. I WON'T ACCEPT ANYTHING LESS THAN AN A STAR. I THINK THAT'S WHAT PEOPLE AROUND ME THINK ABOUT ME. I ALSO FEEL LIKE I HAVE TO LIVE UP TO THAT EXPECTATION NOW. THAT'S WHY I ALSO WORK SO HARD TO TRY AND GET THOSE GRADES. I'M NOT SURE WHAT I'M GOING TO COME BACK WITH, BUT I DID MY PART, I DID MY BEST."

Emma Raducanu

Emma sat the last of her exams in April 2021, bringing her days at Newstead Wood to a close. Emma had been there for seven years and, while it hadn't always been easy balancing her life between school and tennis, she made friends there and was glad she and her parents made the decision for her to stay on, saying:

"I THINK STAYING IN SCHOOL HAS DEFINITELY HELPED ME IN TERMS OF HAVING ANOTHER SET OF FRIENDS I CAN COME INTO. IT WAS A DIFFERENT WAY OF LIFE. IT'S A BIT OF AN ESCAPE AS WELL FOR ME. TO HAVE ANOTHER THING GOING ALONGSIDE MY TENNIS, IT'S KEPT MY MIND OCCUPIED."

With her exams over, Emma took her mind off her results by throwing herself back into training. With school and lockdowns, Emma had been away from the competitive circuit for over a year and she was keen to get her career back on track.

Emma stepped back onto the court and into the British Tour at Felixstowe on 24 May 2021. After playing so well in the tour in 2020 Emma entered the main draw of the competition as the top seed. Emma lived up to the high expectations placed on her by winning the title.

In June, Emma made her Women's Tennis Association tour debut at the 2021 Viking Open in Nottingham, United Kingdom. The Viking Open is a WTA 250 event, which means the winner of the tournament received 250 points towards their ranking. Emma entered the competition as a Wild Card in the main draw. She played well, but was knocked out in the first round by fellow Brit Harriet Dart.

WILD CARD

A wild card is an invitation from a tournament's organizers allowing a player who might not ordinarily qualify to compete. Organizers give out wild cards for a number of reasons, such as previously highly ranked players returning from injury, young up-and-coming players who show promise and local players likely to create excitement among fans. A player like Emma would be issued a wild card in the hope that she would help stoke British interest in tennis.

Emma returned to play in the ITF 100k in Nottingham, this time making it all the way through to the quarter finals. She played strongly in the tournament and impressed members of the All England Lawn Tennis and Croquet Club who manage the Wimbledon Championships. Before Nottingham, Emma had already been given a wild card for the qualifying rounds, as she had in previous years. But, after seeing her play so well, the All England Lawn Tennis and Croquet Club upgraded her wild card straight to Wimbledon's main draw.

A WILD RIDE
AT WIMBLEDON

T his was a dream come true for Emma. All tennis players, particularly British ones, dream of playing at and one day winning Wimbledon. Emma had taken part in qualifying rounds before, but hadn't quite made it through. Now, with her wild card, she would be in the main draw, playing against the world's highest ranking players. Emma had been given a big chance and she wanted to make the most out of it and prove she was worthy of the opportunity.

Due to COVID-19 restrictions, Emma and the other players, trainers and officials had to stay in special accommodation and limit their contact with people who weren't directly involved with the tournament. This was called a bubble.

"WHEN I WAS PACKING
TO COME INTO THE BUBBLE
MY PARENTS WERE LIKE,
'AREN'T YOU PACKING
TOO MANY PAIRS OF
MATCH KIT?'"

Emma Raducanu

WILD CARD WINNER!

Even though tournament organizers issue wild
cards in the hope a player will do well, it is
still highly unlikely that a player will go on to
win. In fact, only one wild card player has ever
gone on to win the Wimbledon Championships.
In 2001, men's tennis player, Goran Ivanisevic
won the Wimbledon Championship after being
given a wild card entry into the tournament.
Ivanisevic was ranked 125 in the world at

the time. He had suffered some setbacks in his career after having made it to the finals at Wimbledon three times before, but had not managed to win the title. In 2001, Ivanisevic played one of Wimbledon's most memorable finals becoming the first and only wild card entry ever to win the championship.

Emma did not have anywhere near as much experience at the other players in the tournament, nor did she have the ranking, but one advantage she did have over most of the competition was a home crowd, rooting for her to do her best.

Round One

Emma's first game was on 30 June against 31-year-old Russian player Vitalia Diatchenko. It was the most important game in her career. There was a lot of pressure and she wanted more than anything to do well, but it didn't start out that way. Emma is known for her powerful serve that can put her opponent on the defensive, but sometimes power can be hard to control. In Emma's first service game of the match she served four double faults, handing the game to her opponent. In the first set, Emma had to fight hard in every game, but after five games it was four games to one to Diatchenko who looked likely to take the set.

It was only her first set in the tournament, but already Emma faced a difficult point in the match. A few errors or missed shots could mean she would lose the set and make it even harder for herself. It would have been easy for her to panic, or lose sight of her belief in herself, but Emma did not. This was a crunch moment. The kind of moment she had practised and prepared for with her coaches back at Bromley and the London Tennis Centre. Emma put the lost games and double faults behind her and started afresh looking at the game ahead.

Emma fought back from four games down to take the set and, with that boost, she blitzed her way through the second set without losing a game to make it through to the next round.

Round Two

Emma's next game was against Czech player Marketa Vondrousova. Marketa was only 22 but had played in many Grand Slam Tournaments and was ranked 35 in the world. Emma, who was just starting out, was only 338. But Emma had never struggled with numbers. She loved maths and this problem she could solve with her tennis racket. Her powerful serve helped Emma to win her service games in the first set, and her big returns helped her to break Marketa's. Emma took the first set six games to two. Heading into the second set, Emma looked like she would be able to win the match without too much of a problem, but unfortunately she wasn't the only player to have prepared for crunch moments. Marketa had been in difficult spots before and she used her experience to fight back, soon leaving Emma three games down in the second set, but Marketa couldn't keep it up. Emma held her nerve as Marketa started to make mistakes and took the set and the match.

From never having played in the main draw

of a Grand Slam tournament, Emma had made it through to the third round. By doing so, she earned £115,000 in prize money. But making it through to the third round didn't just earn her prize money, it also got people's attention. People who had never heard of Emma before now knew her name and wanted to watch her play and see her triumph. Emma was glad of the support, but with more attention came more pressure. Emma was the only British women's singles player to make it to the third round that year. Playing and doing well had meant a lot to Emma, her family and her team before, but it hadn't been a big deal for anyone else. Now it felt like Emma's performance in the tournament mattered to the whole country.

"SOMEONE HAS TO BE IN THE SECOND WEEK, WHY NOT ME?"

Emma Raducanu

Round Three

Emma's third round match was against Romanian player Sorana Cirstea and took place on Court One in front of a large crowd. Emma was playing better than she had ever done in her life. Every time she won a point the crowd erupted in cheers of support. After a long rally in which Emma flew across the court, Emma won, falling to her knees in disbelief. It was Emma's first Wimbledon, her first Grand Slam Tournament and one of her first major tournament since the world had shut down a year before and neither she nor anyone else could believe how well it was going.

People watching wondered if they could be seeing a future British Champion; a player who could end their long wait to see a British woman lift the singles trophy again, something they hadn't seen since Virginia Wade won in 1977.

PLAYER PROFILE: VIRGINIA WADE

Born: 10 July 1945, Bournemouth
Nationality: British
Height: 5' 7"
Plays: Right-handed
Highest WTA ranking: 2

Virginia Wade learned to play tennis growing up in South Africa and continued to play after moving to the United Kingdom, playing for her school team at Wimbledon County Girls Grammar School. When Virginia started her tennis career, women's tennis was considered an amateur game unlike the men's and it was hard to make a living as a player.

In 1968, Virginia Wade won the very first Women's Singles title at the US open, beating the player instrumental in setting up the tournament, Billie Jean King (see page 153).

Virginia also won the Australian Open in 1972, but a win at Wimbledon proved elusive. Wade played in fifteen Wimbledon Championships, managing to make it through to the quarter and semi-finals more than once, but winning always seemed to be out of her reach. Virginia won the championship to cries of 'Come on Ginny!' on her sixteenth attempt in 1977, during the tournament's 100th anniversary. Virginia's trophy was presented by Her Majesty, Queen Elizabeth, who watched the match from the Royal Box.

Wade retired from professional tennis in 1985 and went on to become a regular sports reporter and commentator for the BBC.

"I AM GOING TO WIN THIS YEAR. THE QUEEN'S COMING."

Virginia Wade, 1977

Emma had made it through to the fourth round. Newspapers were filled with stories of her 'astonishing talent' and what a 'delightful tale' her rise from obscurity was.

In the space of just four days, Emma had gone from a promising young tennis player who had just completed her A-levels to a household name. She was playing against athletes she had watched at home, long before she had the chance of playing somewhere like Wimbledon. She tried not to let this worry her. She was having fun feeding off the positive energy of the crowd, saying:

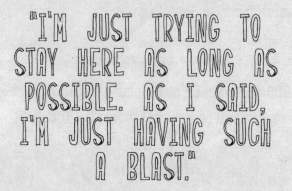

"I'M JUST TRYING TO STAY HERE AS LONG AS POSSIBLE. AS I SAID, I'M JUST HAVING SUCH A BLAST."

Emma hadn't prepared to be in the fourth round. Even though her parents thought she had packed more than she needed to, the night before the match Emma had to send her tennis whites to the hotel laundry.

Round Four

Although Emma arrived looking ready, after the first few games against Australian Ajla Tomljanovic, she started to look uncomfortable. They were under the Court One roof and it was

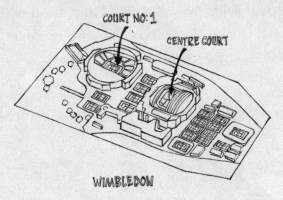

louder and hotter than her previous games. The crowd was also bigger. Whereas Emma was used to playing in front of perhaps a hundred or so people there were many more packed inside the stadium and millions watching from home.

While many players have years to gradually

adjust to playing in high-pressure tournaments, Emma had skyrocketed onto Court One and into the media spotlight in a matter of days.

At the start of the second set, it was obvious that Emma was struggling. She was holding her stomach and looked like she was struggling to breathe. The long rallies at the end of the first set made it hard for her to regain her composure. She signalled to speak with her trainer. Emma needed medical help. She was advised to pull out of the match as it would not be safe for her continue. It was a devastating decision. She later said,

"I WAS PLAYING THE BEST TENNIS OF MY LIFE IN FRONT OF AN AMAZING CROWD THIS WEEK AND I THINK THE WHOLE EXPERIENCE CAUGHT UP WITH ME."

Emma continued: "At the end of the first set, after some super intense rallies, I started to breathe heavily and felt dizzy. The medical team advised me not to continue and although it felt like the hardest thing in the world not to be able to finish my Wimbledon on the court, I was not well enough to carry on."

Everybody seemed to have an opinion on why Emma had retired from the match. Even people with little experience of playing any sport or doing anything at an elite level. Some even claimed it was due to her lacking the mental toughness it took to be a champion. These voices were soon drowned out by fellow tennis players and people with experience of playing high-pressure sports.

While Emma was disappointed and worried that she had let people down, she didn't let what happened take away from the incredible experience she had just had, saying:

"LAST NIGHT WILL GO A LONG WAY TO HELPING ME

LEARN WHAT IT TAKES TO PERFORM AT THE TOP. I WILL CHERISH EVERYTHING WE HAVE ACHIEVED TOGETHER THIS WEEK AND COME BACK STRONGER! CAN'T WAIT TO SEE WHAT'S NEXT ON MY JOURNEY."

Wimbledon had been a wild experience and Emma's first taste of elite level tennis. While she may have fallen at the final hurdle, she had proven that she had the skills to compete and now had a ranking to match. Emma's success pushed her ranking up from 338 to 175.

Throughout her career, Emma had put tough spots and difficult moments aside to focus on what was ahead and now was no different. Her ability to move on and recover was one of her greatest strengths. Emma and her family set her sights on what was next, and for Emma that was a series of tournaments in the USA.

On 2 August, Emma played in the Silicon Valley Classic in San Jose, followed a week later by Koser Jeweler Challenge, an ITF 100 tournament in Pennsylvania. Emma made it all the way through to the quarter final. While in Pennsylvania, Emma found out her results from her A-levels. Emma was awarded an A* in Maths and an A in economics. With the results she wanted in hand, Emma could now focus solely on tennis.

After Pennsylvania, Emma travelled to Chicago to take part in the WTA Chicago Women's open, making it all the way to the final. Emma was playing in a way she hadn't been able to before, travelling from tournament to tournament without having to think about juggling school assignments or exams, but that didn't mean she wasn't being tested. In fact, Emma was about to face a big test, her second Grand Slam Tournament – the US Open at Flushing Meadows, New York.

START SPREADING THE NEWS

When Emma arrived in New York, she didn't think she would be staying there long. She was thrilled to be taking part in the second Grand Slam Tournament of her career, but she had booked her flight home for the end of qualifying rounds, thinking she would be knocked out of the tournament at an early stage. Emma had been in America for a while and was ready to get back to Bromley and her family and friends. Emma's mum and dad didn't think Emma would be in New York very long either. They had not travelled with Emma due to visa and COVID-19 travel restrictions, and while they could have applied for a waiver, there seemed little point in doing everything that was necessary to get there just to watch one or maybe two qualifying matches.

Against the Odds

Emma and her parents weren't being pessimistic. No player had ever made it through via qualifying in a Grand Slam and gone on to win the title. They have never even made it to the semi-finals. That was just a fact. To make it, Emma would have to win ten straight matches, and even though she was playing excellent tennis and her ranking was now 150, such a feat was very unlikely. Despite Emma's wonderful run at Wimbledon, no one expected what happened next.

Great Qualifications

Emma's first qualifying match was on 25 August against thirty-three-year-old Bibiane Schoofs from the Netherlands. This was Emma's first match in a major overseas tournament, but if she was nervous, she showed no sign of it when she stepped on court. The match lasted only sixty-one minutes and Emma only lost three games to win the match 6:1, 6:2.

Emma's next match the following day against

Georgian, Mariam Bolkvadze, was tougher. Both players served well, and Emma wasn't able to break Bolkvadze's until the seventh game. After the break, Emma went on to win the next two games to take the set. It was hot on court and her opponent was fierce, but Emma stayed calm and focused on the match ahead. The second set was even tougher, but Emma held her serve and waited for an opportunity to break her opponent's. Emma won the match 6:3, 7:5 in just over an hour and thirty minutes.

Emma's third qualifying round was against Egyptian, Mayar Sherif, ranked 95 in the world. Emma could feel herself improving with every game she played against the high-level opponents she was playing against. She was learning from every opportunity and putting everything she learned into lethal strokes across the court. Emma's work on her ground strokes shone in the match, her strong two-handed backhand often proving too much for Mayar. Emma reached the ball early and sent it to the far corners of the court, beyond the reach of her opponent. Her game was ruthless and her opponent struggled to fight back. Emma broke Mayar's serve early and after just 22 minutes of play was winning five games to zero. Emma took the first set 6:1 and while Mayar fought back harder in the second set, Emma held her serve and won 6:4 to take the match and progress through to the main draw of the tournament.

Emma had made it through qualifying and into the main draw of a Grand Slam tournament. This was a first for Emma, even though she had made it through to the fourth round at Wimbledon, she had entered the main draw via a wild card. For Emma this made a big difference. This time she had made it through all by herself.

"IT IS DEFINITELY A VERY NICE FEELING HAVING ACHIEVED IT ON MY OWN."

Emma Raducanu

Emma was excited after each win and relied on her team to help calm her down. Outside of the tournament, her name was trending on social media once again. Emma was aware of the attention, but did her best to steer clear of her phone. Instead, she focused on resting, keeping herself in tip-top shape with her coach and her physio. She had three days to recover from her qualifying matches and be ready for what was ahead.

Main Draw

Emma's first round match on 31 August, was against Swiss player Stefanie Voegele. Emma's calm focused approach to her previous matches had worked. She decided to use the same approach again. In the first set, Emma held her serve and broke down her opponent with fast returns and her speed across the court. Emma's confident performance continued into the second set, which looked like it would fall to her as easily, until it came to match point. Even though she was so close to winning, Emma's nerves had started to get to her. To win a game of tennis a player has to win by two points, and while Emma had done this many times, when it came to the final point she didn't seem to have the confidence to put away her opponent. Emma fought six match points before regaining her poise to finally defeat Voegele.

After a day off to rest, Emma played her second-round match on 2 September against Shuai Zhang from China. Emma took the first set 6:2 and while Zhang fought back in the second set, Emma did not lose her nerve. Serving at match point Emma stayed close to the base line to meet Zhang's return. Emma controlled the play as Zhang flew around the court trying to get her racket to the ball, eventually sending a forehand shot that landed just outside the line sending Emma into the next round.

Emma was through to the third round of a Grand Slam without having lost a single set. She was playing the best tennis of her life and with every game and match that she won, her confidence grew. She brought this confidence to the court against Spanish player Sara Sorribes Tormo. Sorribes Tormo had been tipped to win, but Emma dominated from the beginning. She won the match in just over an hour, losing only a single game out of the thirteen games played.

Fourth Round

Emma had made it as far as she had at Wimbledon before she'd had to retire. Up until this point in the tournament, she had played her matches in front of smaller crowds at the Billie Jean King Tennis Center. While these held more people than she was used to, they were nothing compared to the Arthur Ashe Stadium where the fourth round was held. This tennis stadium, the biggest in the world, could hold 23,771 spectators.

PLAYER PROFILE: ARTHUR ASHE

Born: 10 July 1943, Richmond, Virginia, USA

Nationality: American

Height: 6' 1"

Plays: Right-handed

Highest ranking: 1

Arthur Ashe began playing tennis when he was seven and became such a good player he earned

ARTHUR ASHE

a scholarship to go to college. After serving in the army for two years in 1966, Arthur Ashe became the first black man to be selected for the US Davis Cup team, helping them to victory in 1968, 1969 and 1970.

While still an amateur player, Arthur Ashe won the first ever men's singles title at the US Open in 1968 and was the first black man to win a Grand Slam tournament. He then became the first black man to win the Australian Open in 1970 and the first to win Wimbledon in 1975. That same year he also reached his highest rank of number one.

As well as being a talented tennis player, Arthur Ashe was also a human rights activist, speaking out against the treatment of black people in South Africa.

Ashe retired from professional tennis in 1979 due to a heart condition. The 23,771 seater stadium at Flushing, New York, was opened in 1997 in his honour.

"SUCCESS IS A JOURNEY, NOT A DESTINATION. THE DOING IS OFTEN MORE IMPORTANT THAN THE OUTCOME."

The fourth round crowd was huge, and not only that, unlike Wimbledon, when she was on home turf, Emma was up against American player, Shelby Rogers, in front of her own home crowd. Rogers had made it to the quarter final of the tournament the year before and was keen to make it even further this year.

But Emma had enough supporters of her own. Her meteoric rise through the tournament had captured the imaginations of tennis fans in the USA just as it had at Wimbledon. Everyone wanted to see Emma play her best.

The match did not start well for Emma. Serving the first game, she soon found herself 40-love down. A break this early on would be difficult to come back from. This was a crunch moment like the ones she had trained for. Emma put the lost points behind her to put pressure on her opponent, taking back the game, the set and eventually the match and winning herself a place in the quarter finals.

Any concerns that she didn't have the mental strength to play at the highest levels of the sport had been silenced. Emma still felt the nerves and had shown them on court, but she had found ways to pull herself through those moments, focus on what she needed to do and keep going. She had won seven matches and not lost a single set, she had played on a stiflingly hot court with the capacity of 23,771 and played an opponent with a home crowd behind them and she had triumphed. Emma knew how unlikely her rise had been and knew that she had nothing to lose at this stage in the tournament. She had already done more and played far better than anyone had expected. Anything she managed to do now was a bonus.

The Final Eight

The quarter final promised to be Emma's toughest match in the competition so far. She was up against Olympic Gold medallist and world number 12, Belinda Bencic, from Switzerland.

It took time for Emma to settle into the game. The pair were well matched, playing long rallies at each point but as Emma became familiar with Bencic's rhythm of play and the timing of her ball strike, she found a way to fight back aggressively to take the first set. Emma kept up the pressure until she was serving for the match at five games to four. But Bencic was fighting back. Soon Emma was love thirty down with Bencic about to break her serve. If Bencic took the game, Emma would have to win two games to claim victory. She needed to stay calm. Emma reset herself and focused on what she could control, blocking out everything else. Emma knew what patterns she was going to play and fixed her mind on them.

It worked. She launched a forceful backhand to the baseline, and although Bencic got a racket to it she was unable to control her return, sending it into the net and Emma into the semi-final.

At just 18 years old, and playing in only her second major tournament, Emma had become the only player in history to make it through from the qualifying rounds of a Grand Slam to the semi-final. In the press conference after the match Emma said she wasn't looking to break any records but just focusing on the things she could control, though she did find it cool when she found out that after her performance so far in the tournament she would be the number one women's single player in Great Britain.

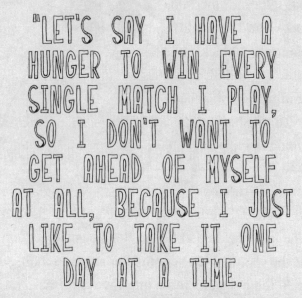

"LET'S SAY I HAVE A HUNGER TO WIN EVERY SINGLE MATCH I PLAY, SO I DON'T WANT TO GET AHEAD OF MYSELF AT ALL, BECAUSE I JUST LIKE TO TAKE IT ONE DAY AT A TIME.

Emma Raducanu

Emma went on: "If I take care of what I can control, then that's going to give me the best chance. Until now, I think it's worked very well for me not getting ahead of myself, just focusing on one point at a time. It's got me to this stage, and I'm not going to change anything."

Emma wasn't the only teenager to make it through to the semi-final, a Canadian player named Leylah Fernandez had also enjoyed a successful tournament. In the press conference after the match Emma said they had played before and knew each other from coming up through the game at the Orange Bowl and also junior Wimbledon. Emma said she was glad she was in the tournament not least because Leylah had been handing out cupcakes the day before.

Semi Final

Emma used the next day to do what she always did in a busy tournament: rest and prepare for the next match.

The semi-final was against world number seventeen Maria Sakkari, from Greece. Emma knew she had to play aggressively against such an experienced and high ranked opponent. It was the biggest match of Emma's career so far, but Emma was getting used to playing those. She used her big serve and strong ground strokes to break Maria's second service game and then carried on to win five straight games to take the first set. Emma used the same winning formula in the second, breaking Maria's serve and taking the second set six games to four. The crowd in the Arthur Ashe stadium went wild. Emma, a teenage qualifier was through to the final of one of the biggest tournaments in the world. People couldn't believe what they were seeing, and neither could Emma who said, "I personally think inside I knew I had some sort of level inside of me that was similar to these girls, but I didn't know if I was able to maintain it over a set or over two sets. To be able to do it and play the best players in the world and beat them, I honestly can't believe it."

She had an incredible run. Following her performances up to the quarter final, her ranking had stormed all the way up to 54. In many ways the pressure was off. She had done far more than she came to do and far exceeded what anyone expected of her. Emma found this feeling freeing.

When asked if she felt any pressure going into the final, she answered:

"IS THERE ANY EXPECTATION? I AM THE QUALIFIER ... THERE'S NO PRESSURE."

"HONESTLY, THE TIME HERE IN NEW YORK HAS JUST GONE SO FAST, I'VE JUST BEEN TAKING CARE OF EACH DAY AND BEFORE YOU KNOW IT, I'M IN THE FINAL AND I CAN'T ACTUALLY BELIEVE IT."

A TEENAGE DREAM

Canadian Leylah Fernandez had also made it to the final. Nineteen-year-old, Leylah's rise through the US Open had been almost as exciting as Emma's, beating three of the top five seeds on her way to the final including 2020 US Open Champion, Naomi Osaka, in a tense three set match in the third round. The final promised to be an exciting match and was the first all-teenage final in over twenty years, since Serena Williams won against Martina Hingis in 1999.

"I think it shows that the future of women's tennis and the depth of the women's game is so great," Raducanu said. She went on:

"EVERY SINGLE PLAYER IN THE WOMEN'S DRAW HAS A SHOT TO WIN THE

TOURNAMENT. LET'S HOPE
THE NEXT GENERATION CAN
FOLLOW IN THE FOOTSTEPS
OF SOME OF THE LEGENDS,
LIKE BILLIE JEAN KING."

BILLIE JEAN KING AND THE WOMEN'S TENNIS ASSOCIATION

Growing up, Billie Jean King was brilliant at almost every sport she took up. She started playing tennis aged eleven and went on to win a total of 39 Grand Slams – twelve singles and twenty-seven doubles titles.

During her career, Billie became frustrated that some tournaments were only open to men, and that tournaments in which women were allowed to compete, including Wimbledon, only offered a fraction of the prize money available to men. To fight this, in 1970, Billie Jean King gathered a group of eight tennis players together to set up their own women's tennis tour. It was a risk and could have caused the players to be banned from other tournaments, but it paid off.

In 1973, Billie founded the Women's Tennis Association (WTA) to bring together all women players in a single tour. The effect of uniting all women in a single association put pressure on tournaments to improve the prize money offered to women players and, ideally, match the prize money offered to men. In 1973, the US Open became the first Grand Slam tournament to do just that.

Billie retired in 1990. Since then, she has remained closely tied to tennis and the organization she set up, as well as continuing the fight for equal rights. Today, the Women's Tennis Association (WTA) represents 1,650 players in eighty-five countries.

In 2006, the USTA National Tennis Center was renamed the USTA Billie Jean King National Tennis Center in recognition of her contribution to the sport.

BILLIE JEAN KING

Emma was determined to take her shot, but Leylah was determined too. One of Leylah's aims for 2021 was to end the year ranked in the top-10 women's singles players. A win at the US Open would put her well on the way to achieving her goal.

PLAYER PROFILE: LEYLAH FERNANDEZ

Born: 6 September 2002, Montreal, Canada

Nationality: Canadian

Height: 5' 6"

Plays: Left-handed

Highest WTA ranking: 27

Leylah first started playing tennis in her driveway where she would do her best not to damage the family car before moving on to hitting the ball against the basement wall and trying to avoid destroying the television. Eventually Leylah had tennis lessons at her local club and as she got older was coached by her father, Jorge a former professional football player. Leylah's first ITF Tournament was in October 2016 at the Shipyard Cup at Hilton Head Island, South Carolina.

Emma looked calm and relaxed as she began the match. She served confidently in the first game and controlled play. As Emma won her service game in the first set, the commentator compared her play to her hero Li Na in her composure and talent for blocking out the noise around her to focus on the game. Emma then fought to break Leylah's first service game. Her opponent made it hard for her, but Emma kept up the pressure and took the second game. The first set looked likely to fall to Emma, but Leylah didn't give up. Instead, she broke Emma's serve right back. They were well matched, taking balls early and making each other work for every point.

Emma found it tough to get used to the rhythm of Leylah's play, but stayed calm and focused on each point. She had won five games to Leylah's four. Emma needed to break Leylah's serve to take the match, but Leylah wasn't going to give up without a fight. She defended three set points. Emma triumphed by sending a forehand out of Leylah's reach and taking the first set.

Emma threw her arms up into the air and yelled as the crowd cheered. So far, she had managed not to get ahead of herself, but here she was, one set up in the final of the US Open. Among the cheering crowd of more than 23,000 people were tennis greats such as Tim Henman, Virginia Wade and Billie Jean King.

Millions more were watching at home. Emma was one step away from winning her first ever Grand Slam tournament. Her life had already changed for ever, but just how much it would now change was between her and Leylah Fernandez to decide.

Both players went into the second set prepared to fight it out. Leylah looked composed and although Emma broke her first service game, she broke Emma's right back. The noise of the crowd was deafening. It had been a game of epic rallies with Emma running and sliding across the court. During one of her slides Emma fell, cutting open her knee. She had to see a medic to stop the bleeding. She was winning five sets to three and was serving to win the match and worried that stopping play at such a crucial moment would affect her composure but she didn't have a choice. According to US Open rules, if a player is bleeding, they have to see a medic for treatment. Medics have five minutes to get the situation under control. Thankfully for Emma they worked fast and she was able to get up and resume play before the time expired.

Emma won the match with an ace. And fell to the ground with her head in her hands, not quite able to believe what she had just done. Once she recovered Emma ran off the court to go and see her team in the stands including Andrew Richardson who had first coached an eleven-year-old Emma Raducanu. This was the team who had helped bring her through the tournament, who had kept her calm between matches and made sure she was ready to meet whatever she faced on court.

ANDREW RICHARDSON

A Dream Come True

Emma's trophy was presented by Billie Jean King. Billie had enjoyed the match and watching such young players succeed. She later tweeted:

"WHAT A TERRIFIC DISPLAY OF COMPETITION AND MATURITY FROM TWO EXCEPTIONAL PLAYERS. IT IS WONDERFUL TO SEE THIS GENERATION LIVING OUR DREAM. I CAN'T REMEMBER THE US OPEN WITH BETTER CROWD SUPPORT. THANK YOU NY, THE GREATEST FANS IN THE WORLD. AND CONGRATULATIONS, EMMA!"

It was a dream come true for Emma. The trophy was engraved with the names of all the previous winners and now hers would join them. Emma lifted the trophy into the air as ribbons cascaded onto the court.

In the press conference after the match Emma was asked if she was surprised by how easy her win had been, having played ten matches without dropping a set. Emma said that although it looked easy on paper each of the matches had been very tough and although she had not dropped a set, she had had to fight to win every game.

After the match and the interview, Emma travelled back to the hotel in a party bus and sang *Sweet Caroline* with her team. Back at the hotel they stayed up late talking and reflecting on the incredible journey they had been on.

"WE ALL SPENT THE NIGHT JUST REFLECTING AND IT WAS A REALLY COOL MOMENT BECAUSE IT'S BEEN

SUCH A LONG TRIP FOR US AND EVERYTHING HAS GONE SO FAST. WE JUST GOT TO REFLECT AND SHARE A FEW STORIES AND IT WAS A REALLY NICE NIGHT TO HAVE WITH EVERYONE."

Emma Raducanu

Emma didn't go wild with the $2.5 million prize money either. In fact when asked what she planned to do with it she claimed that to help motivate herself on court she had told herself, "If I win my match today, I can buy a new set of AirPods." Emma could buy a lot more than that. Even if she had not won the tournament, the prize for the runner up was $1.75 million, more than enough for some AirPods and a couple of houses to keep them in.

SAY HELLO TO
EMMA RADUCANU

Emma would get plenty of time to celebrate over the following days. What happened after the tournament was almost as spectacular as the win itself. Emma's story inspired people and catapulted her into the media spotlight. Her phone exploded with messages and she was sent congratulations from friends and famous people including British Prime Minister, Boris Johnson, and Her Majesty Queen Elizabeth whose message was posted on the official royal website:

"I send my congratulations to you on your success in winning the United States Open Tennis Championships. It is a remarkable achievement at such a young age, and is testament to your hard work and dedication. I have no doubt your outstanding performance, and that of your opponent Leylah Fernandez, will inspire the next generation of tennis players.

I send my warmest good wishes to you and your many supporters."

The prime minister tweeted, "What a sensational match! Huge congratulations to Emma Raducanu. You showed extraordinary skill, poise and guts and we are all hugely proud of you." While the Duchess of Cambridge said, "Huge congratulations @EmmaRaducanu on your stunning performances and historic Grand Slam victory! Incredible – we are all so proud of you. @LeylahFernandez well done on your amazing achievements at this year's #USOpen, it's been a pleasure to watch."

Emma's social media following exploded too and television channels fought to get her into their studios or to appear virtually on their shows. Everyone wanted to know more about how Emma felt about such a landmark victory and how she had managed to achieve such success at such a young age.

Emma's parents hadn't been able travel to New York for the tournament, but they had been watching at home. Emma made sure to let the world know how instrumental their support had been in getting to where she found herself.

"I think that from a young age I've always sort of been brought up to have mental strength," she told the presenter George Stephanopoulos. "My parents played a huge part in my upbringing and they were pretty tough on me when I was young, but it kind of shaped the way I am."

Ball Girl

As part of the celebrations Emma was invited to attend the Met Gala in New York by Vogue Editor-in-Chief, Anna Wintour. To get ready for the star-studded event, Emma was moved from her room at the player hotel, to a suite in the luxurious Peninsular Hotel on 5th Avenue. There she was treated to professional hair and make-up and got to choose from a selection of Chanel gowns. Emma was suddenly rubbing shoulders with celebrities including Formula One Champion, Lewis Hamilton, Billie Eilish and Pharrell Williams.

"THE MET WAS SUCH AN ARTISTIC EVENT WITH GREAT PERFORMANCES AND I WAS VERY HONOURED AND GRATEFUL TO HAVE BEEN ABLE TO GO."

Emma the Brand

Suddenly Emma was everywhere. On television, in newspapers, magazines, blogs and even several stories high on a digital billboard in Times Square in New York. The world was watching, which meant brands were keen to associate themselves with Emma, her story and her success.

Going into the tournament Emma had a deal with Nike and Wilson to wear their clothes and use their equipment. It is estimated that these deals were worth £100,000 per year but that they would now be increased in line with her success. On top of this, other brands wanted her to endorse their products including fashion and jewellery companies such as Tiffany. Thankfully Emma had signed with an agent to help negotiate these deals on her behalf.

Homecoming Queen

Emma's new superstar treatment lasted until just after she landed in London where she was greeted by fans and given a police escort all the way back to Bromley to protect her from photographers and make sure she arrived safely. At home, Emma finally got to see her parents for a hug. Her mother made her favourite homemade dumplings and the family settled down together to watch a replay of her historic match:

"WHEN I WAS WATCHING IT, IT ALMOST FEELS LIKE THAT'S NOT ME WHO'S PLAYING AND PULLING OFF SOME OF THOSE SHOTS."

While she was growing up, Emma's parents were tough to please. Emma believes this is due to their upbringing and to her mother's Chinese heritage, "My mum has a Chinese background, they have very good self-belief. It's not necessarily about telling everyone how good you are but it's about believing it in yourself. I really respect that about the culture."

Emma's hard work, self-discipline and self-belief had won her the US Open, but had she done enough to please her parents? Emma said:

"THEY ARE MY TOUGHEST CRITICS, AND VERY, VERY HARD TO PLEASE. BUT, YEAH, I GOT THEM WITH THIS ONE."

Back in the United Kingdom, Emma appeared on countless interviews before taking some time to relax and make some decisions about what she wanted to do next, but it wasn't long until she was back training at the London Tennis Centre and trying out new coaches to help her take the next steps in her career.

"ALL THE OPPORTUNITIES I'M GETTING HAVE BEEN VERY FUN, WHERE I REALLY WANT TO BE IS ON A TENNIS COURT BECAUSE I WAS JUST THRIVING OUT THERE."

A Bright Future

As well as focusing on her own future, Emma had teamed up with the LTA to be an ambassador for their youth programme. As part of this, Emma took part in an event to encourage young people to take up the game. Emma took to the court for a friendly double match with the patron of the Lawn Tennis Association, the Duchess of Cambridge. Emma's rise to the top of the game was watched by millions of people all over Great

Britain and prompted record numbers of young people to want to pick up a racket and follow in her footsteps. There is certainly a great deal more to come from Emma's life story and she is sure to inspire many more people to take up tennis before she's through.

GLOSSARY

Amateur In sports, an athlete who competes while still studying or working.

Break of serve When a player wins a game in which their opponent is serving.

Citizenship A person who legally belongs to and is a full member of a country. Citizens give their allegiance to a country and have the rights and protections of that nation.

COVID-19 One of a family of viruses – coronavirus – that sometimes move from animals to humans. COVID-19 is a new virus that affects humans.

Double fault If a player's second serve lands outside of the service box or doesn't clear the net it's known as double fault and they lose the point.

Fault When a player serves, if the ball lands outside of the service box or doesn't clear the net it's a fault. If this happens on a player's first serve they can take a second serve.

Grand Slam This term refers to the accomplishment of a player winning the four most important annual tennis championships in a year year. They are the Australian Open, French Open, US Open and Wimbledon.

International Tennis Federation (ITF) Founded in 1913, the ITF is the governing body of world tennis, wheelchair tennis and beach tennis.

Lawn Tennis Association (LTA) The national governing body for tennis in Great Britain.

'Love' Both players begin a game with zero points, which is know as 'love'.

Pandemic A widespread outbreak of an infectious disease across a whole country or the world.

Patron Someone who provides support to a person, organization or a cause.

Press conference A meeting between the media and an athlete where the media is given time to ask the player questions.

Professional In sports, an athlete who competes in sporting events and receives payment for their performance.

Rally A series of shots between players once a point has begun. A rally continues until a point is scored.

Rating A measuring tool that indicates a player's current ability. A player's rating determines which grade of tournament they can enter. The higher the rating, the higher the grade of tournament.

Seeding The system used to separate the top players in a draw so that they will not meet in the early rounds of a tournament. Usually the seedings match players' rankings, but some tournaments also take other factors into account when deciding on seeds.

Serve A shot that will start a point. Players alternate serving each game.

Service game: a game in which the player is serving.

Sponsor A person or organization who provides financial support to an athlete.

Wild card A player who is awarded a tournament entry at the discretion of the organizers.

Women's Tennis Association (WTA) The worldwide governing body of women's professional tennis.

Virus: A tiny life form that can invade the body, where they multiply and cause illness.